Nietzsche and the
Death of God

Selected Writings

Nietzsche and the Death of God

Selected Writings

translated, edited, and with an introduction by

Peter Fritzsche

University of Illinois at Urbana-Champaign

WAVELAND

PRESS, INC.

Long Grove, Illinois

For information about this book, contact:
Waveland Press, Inc.
4180 IL Route 83, Suite 101
Long Grove, IL 60047-9580
(847) 634-0081
info@waveland.com
www.waveland.com

10-digit ISBN 1-4786-1180-4
13-digit ISBN 978-1-4786-1180-6

Printed in the United States of America

7   6   5   4   3   2   1

Preface

Of the writers and philosophers who have come and gone, Friedrich Nietzsche is one of the few whose texts still have the power to astonish and anger contemporary readers. He has this effect because he relentlessly attacked the little and big conventions that we have fashioned in order to be agreeable to others and to ourselves. Nietzsche repeatedly explored the nature of our attractions and repulsions, our moral codes, and our inclination to stand still rather than to climb over ourselves to find new ways of being in the world. He asked us why we are so incomplete. Nietzsche pushed and prodded, and readers have picked his books up again and again in order to question their sense of familiarity and to prepare for difficult journeys. But Nietzsche wrote many books, and in them, he often digressed as he prowled around the traditions of Western culture. He rewrote as well as wrote, and left a great many half-baked and provisional ideas. Thus, it is difficult to get a coherent idea of Nietzsche's philosophical arguments without considerable work and without switching back from one book to the other. In response, this volume is intended to provide an introduction to Nietzsche's ideas about God, language, truth, and myth—his big themes—and a selection of texts that can be read to provide students with a compact introduction to his major ideas.

The introduction to this collection of Nietzsche's works deals with his life and influence. Separate sections on Nietzsche's importance, ideas, and legacy offer background and historical context and prepare students for the readings that follow. I have selected the documents from the full range of Nietzsche's writings: from the early commentary on "The Uses and Disadvantages of History for Life," to *The Gay Science*, in which Nietzsche's madman makes the riveting announcement of the death of God, to the denser historical analyses in *Beyond*

Good and Evil and *On the Genealogy of Morals,* and to Nietzsche's most popular work, the allegorical *Thus Spoke Zarathustra.* These selections present in an accessible fashion many of the key ideas that Nietzsche developed. In choosing these works, my starting point was the concept of the "death of God," which led Nietzsche to analyze how human beings have created gods, myths, and systems of morality, how they fail to acknowledge this authorship and thus have fallen into a subordinate relationship with creatures of their own making, and how they might come to know themselves as fully creative humans once again. Along the way, Nietzsche introduced his theory of language, which accompanied the rise of society, and his theory of truth, which for Nietzsche is just a workable way of living. From there Nietzsche explored Christian morality and the concept of sin. He pointed out that the victory of any moral code is life-affirming to the extent that it confirms that new things can happen: One victory can be followed by another. This recognition of new possibility is the most important treasure that Nietzsche believed he had excavated. Despite his difficult prose and abstract ideas, Nietzsche is useful for contemplating one's own life because he analyzes why truths and laws have such a hold over people and why it is possible, even desirable, to break that hold.

As an introductory sampling, this collection neglects detailed analyses of ancient Greece, to which Nietzsche returned repeatedly, but which would have required considerable elaboration; highly provocative, but abbreviated reflections on astronomy, mathematics, and nature, although I have included a small sampling; Nietzsche's complicated, somewhat unproductive ideas about eternal recurrence; and his formative relationship with the German composer Richard Wagner. But the purpose of an introduction is to spark further interest, not to provide a comprehensive account, and I hope readers will go out and read more of Nietzsche for themselves. All of Nietzsche's major texts are readily available in English and are listed in the Selected Bibliography at the end of this book.

A number of aids are provided in this volume to help students in their reading of Nietzsche. All of the documents feature headnotes that include publication history and context for the readings that follow. Gloss notes explain literary allusions, historical references, and unfamiliar terms. The appendixes include a chronology of Nietzsche's life, questions for consideration, and a bibliography of selected works by and about Nietzsche.

ACKNOWLEDGMENTS

I am extremely happy to have "my" Nietzsche, and I have come to learn that many people who teach Nietzsche have "their" Nietzsches too. That I was given the opportunity to develop my Nietzsche I owe to Lynn Hunt, who suggested I write this introduction. Lynn also made for a great initial reader. The "German Colloquium" at the University of Illinois read the first draft and made valuable suggestions for improvement. Thanks also to Stephen Brockman. But mostly I am indebted to the excellent reports of the readers: Katherine Aaslestad (West Virginia University), Sidney Bolkosky (University of Michigan–Dearborn), David Imhoof (Susquehanna University), Michele Strong (George Mason University), Deborah Vess (Georgia College & State University), George S. Williamson (University of Alabama), and especially to David Dennis (Loyola University Chicago). My editor, Laura Arcari, did a great job of editing. My wife, Karen, my daughter, Lauren, and my son, Eric, helped proof the translations. This book is dedicated with love to you, Eric.

Peter Fritzsche

A Note about the Text and Translation

The documents included in this volume have been excerpted from longer works. For a listing of the complete works of Nietzsche, please consult the selected bibliography located at the back of this book. The following excerpts are my own translations. Nietzsche is such a well-known writer that it is important to say at the outset where I differ from older, authoritative translations. First, I have translated the German adjective *vornehm* as "refined" rather than "noble," as do Walter Kaufmann and R. J. Hollingdale. I think this is more accurate ("distinguished" is another candidate), avoids confusion when Nietzsche actually refers to the nobility or aristocracy, and keeps readers from overestimating the extent to which Nietzsche thought in terms of a new, almost biological breed of men, which is the case when the noun "noble" is repeatedly used as an adjective. A second note: It is basically impossible to avoid using the collective nouns "man" and "men" and thus also "mankind" when translating Nietzsche. The German language is very gendered to begin with, and Nietzsche was happy to reproduce this gendering. And although "man" excludes, it conveys a kind of fullness of form, which the word "person" simply does not in the context of Nietzsche's arguments. I have also tried to eliminate almost completely the awkward third-person singular "one," which occurs frequently in German, and to replace it with "we" or "you." Finally, the key term *Übermensch* means "person who continuously strives to overcome himself or herself" and is thus quite accurately translated as "overman," although I have retained the less awkward, but much more arresting, "superman." A final note: Ellipses with no brackets indicate the ellipses in Nietzsche's original documents; ellipses in brackets indicate my deletions within Nietzsche's texts.

Contents

APPENDIXES

PART ONE

Introduction:
Nietzsche's Life
and Works

NIETZSCHE'S IMPORTANCE

"Danger: dynamite." This is how one Swiss reviewer believed Friedrich Nietzsche's 1886 work, *Beyond Good and Evil*, should have been labeled: "with black warning flags," just like the "dynamite used to build the Gotthard train tunnel."[1] The very title of the book indicates the audacious scale of Nietzsche's philosophy, which examined the basic distinctions of morality, argued that ideas of evil and sin kept men and women from becoming fully human, and urged readers to abandon the herd (as he called society) to make their own lives beyond moral conventions. It is his incendiary criticism of the most basic precepts of public life that makes Nietzsche such an unsettling, compelling philosopher. Declaring the death of God; rejecting Christianity as well as what he considered to be its modern-day successors— liberalism, democracy, and socialism—as moralities of the weak; characterizing all moral codes to be lies; and finally conjuring up the idea of the "superman" to redeem individuals willing to explore life fully, Nietzsche stands out as a furious, explosive, "black-flagged" thinker who repeatedly pulled apart the certainties of the Western tradition.

Almost completely unknown when he went insane, probably as a result of syphilis, and stopped writing in 1889, Nietzsche did not emerge as a dominant figure in European thought until his death eleven years later. With his declaration that "God is dead," which is a provocative statement even alongside the bathroom-stall rejoinder "Nietzsche is dead," and with his ideal of the superman, who in the 1930s not only influenced fascist thought in Germany but also flew into the United States as the comic-strip figure Superman, Nietzsche is probably the most recognizable modern philosopher. He celebrated the "Dionysian" side of life expressed in myth, dance, and music; wandered the mountaintops of the Swiss Alps; wrote compulsively in dingy hotel rooms; and finally, in 1889, went incurably mad at the age of forty-four at the sight of a man beating a horse on the streets of Turin. With his walruslike moustache, Friedrich Nietzsche seems to epitomize the stereotypical image of a philosopher.

But a closer look reveals that he was anything but typical. As the Austrian writer Stefan Zweig recalls, Nietzsche's was a solitude from which even God was excluded. Born in 1844 in the small village of Röcken, in Saxony, Friedrich Nietzsche was only four when his father died, and he reenacted this death many times by repeatedly removing himself from society. While Nietzsche remained affectionate to his mother and sister, he kept his emotional and intellectual distance, and as a philosopher, never felt understood by them. Instead, Nietzsche spoke approvingly of leaving home and of repudiating tradition. Raised as the son of a pastor, whose vocation he was supposed to follow, Nietzsche felt comfortable with a life of study and contemplation. Nonetheless he completely abandoned the faith of his father, the respect for church and state institutions, and the pieties of small-town life; when he was just in high school, this son and grandson of pastors announced that he was an atheist. Nietzsche enjoyed early successes, studying Greek philology in Leipzig and winning a university post in Basel, Switzerland, at the startlingly young age of twenty-four, only to abandon the professorship, partly out of boredom, partly for his health, for an insecure, restless, and often downright miserable existence as an independent writer.

Nietzsche never made a home, living in the 1870s and 1880s in sparsely furnished boarding rooms as he moved from Sorrento to Nice to Genoa to Turin, returning repeatedly to the Swiss Alps and especially to the mountains and lakes near Sils Maria, Switzerland, and writing with difficulty but without rest the ten or so books that make up his oeuvre before his nervous breakdown in Turin, Italy, in 1889 and his death in his sister's house in Weimar, Germany, in 1900. He lived in pain most of his life, could hardly see, and took a variety of medicines for stomach cramps and insomnia; indeed, his writings are preoccupied with the theme of suffering, although he prized it as a means to a stronger, better life. A sick man, he imagined superman; a solitary man, he welcomed new creatures, "good Europeans," blond beasts, and, above all, the newborn; a brooding man, he embraced cheerfulness and "the great Yes to life."[2]

Nietzsche had little intellectual influence in his lifetime: His "drama was played to a finish before empty seats."[3] In turn, very little of the noise of the nineteenth century penetrated Nietzsche's texts. Readers get few clues to the vast migrations that pushed Europeans into cities and across the oceans for better lives, or the clamorous political movements that mobilized nationalists, liberals, and socialists, or the heave of machinery that remade into iron and steel the physical face of the continent. Nonetheless, his writings are set against the emergence of mass society: the erosion of religious tradition and the rise of public opinion, the growth of the media and the importance of cultural and intellectual fashion, the expansion of the labor market, the call for social reform in cities and factories, and the individual quest for a better life. Whether they were Marxists or liberals or conservatives, nineteenth-century intellectuals participated energetically in debates about the nature of Europe's tumultuous transformation, believed in the ability of Europeans to improve their lives, and advocated one or another solution to the problems of the day. Social criticism and social commentary proliferated. Nietzsche, by contrast, removed himself completely from these debates, which he took as symptoms of increasingly standardized thinking that took as its object the well-being of society instead of the potential of the individual. Wherever he looked, in newspapers, in universities, and in parliaments, Nietzsche saw complacency and uniformity. Imperialism abroad and nationalism at home were as much the evidence of the "herd instinct" in modern society as the desire for creature comforts and the push for social reform or democratic rights. At an abstract level, he blasted away at the British utilitarians and their ideas of beneficial service to the greater majority, which Nietzsche believed characterized modern attitudes. But Nietzsche was occasionally quite concrete in his loathings, especially for the overbearing arrogance and cheap anti-Semitism that emerged in Germany after unification in 1871. In many ways, Nietzsche appears to be a cranky conservative in his distaste for the urban life and democratic pursuits of the nineteenth century. But in one important respect he was a radical: He used the methods of science to explore the nature of the desire for truth and knowledge. In this regard, Nietzsche was a man of the nineteenth century even as he tried to tear it to shreds. It is precisely his estrangement from society and convention and philosophy itself that makes him available to readers long after his death.

Nietzsche's work is intriguing because it is so unfamiliar, and wicked. Nietzsche blasted apart the conventions that regulated social interaction and mocked the public responsibilities of government. He wrote about gods with a passion that his secular, workaday age took to be increasingly obsolescent. At a time when the authority of the sciences to know the world was virtually unquestioned, Nietzsche held all systematic knowledge to be metaphorical, thus erroneous, and ultimately a matter of fancy. If Charles Darwin, Karl Marx, and Sigmund Freud proposed valid laws drawn from the observation of the natural world to apply to human behavior, Nietzsche proposed new worlds of the mind that might still be inhabited. Almost alone among his contemporaries, Nietzsche dismissed the idea that European civilization had discovered the right formulas for success and prosperity, and he urged his readers to see the world with new eyes. He was so radical because he dismissed all the self-satisfaction in scientific progress, rational thought, and technological inventiveness as completely uninteresting. The ideas of self-government, which were debated in various registers by liberals, democrats, and socialists in the one hundred years after the American and French revolutions, Nietzsche condemned as so many ways to make the genuinely "free spirit" submit to social rules and social responsibilities. What contemporaries cherished as the public interest, Nietzsche scorned as the herd. While most nineteenth-century Europeans believed themselves to be at the pinnacle of progress, Nietzsche saw a dead-end.

What makes Nietzsche so influential was his conviction that human beings could regain what made them human if they acknowledged their ability to create the conditions of their life. He saw people as potential masters and lamented that they remained slaves. Rather than talk in "old tongues" or "walk on worn soles,"[4] men and women should leave home for foreign places and see the world with "our own new eyes" (see Document 5, section 143). Nietzsche's most lasting influence is on those individuals who were willing to question "received wisdom." He was avidly taken up by proponents of new lifestyles: anarchists, feminists, and atheists, as well as prophets of religious cults, and, most of all, young people eager to find a distinctive and vital voice for their generation. For the nineteenth century, which prized maturity rather than youth, foundations rather than questions, Nietzsche was explosive, but his thought has beckoned all those on a journey, from the back-to-nature enthusiasts of the pre–World War I youth movements to the riders of the psychedelic-colored Volkswagen buses in the 1960s to punk rockers in more recent years. No other philosopher can claim his wide readership.

Nietzsche's emphasis on new life also appealed to political revolutionaries. Nietzsche hated ideas such as public good and public service because they dictated how people should act (that is, responsibly) and feel (that is, empathetically). Therefore, he repudiated the fundamental premises of liberalism and democracy, which sought to create more fair and equal forms of collective life through law, regulation, and public spirit. He thought that European societies had turned themselves into sickrooms capable of caring for the weak but unable to nurture those wanting to live adventurously. The nineteenth century was particularly odious to him because its inhabitants had come to believe they lived in the very best, most comfortable, and most advanced period imaginable. His ferocious attack on the present condition appealed not so much to socialists and Marxists, who worked inside the Enlightenment tradition, but to political dissidents of a different kind who proliferated in the unsettled decades after World War I: conservatives who rejected democracy's enfranchisement of the masses, aristocrats who despised liberalism's reformist zeal, and nationalists who envisioned a more heroic history. Nietzsche's most notorious political heirs were the Nazis, who in the 1930s frequently quoted the philosopher (with the blessing of his long-lived sister, Elizabeth Förster-Nietzsche, the keeper of Nietzsche's papers) as they constructed the Third Reich and its hierarchies of racial superiors and racial inferiors. Nietzsche remains tainted by their violence and pitilessness.

Nietzsche hated nineteenth-century society for the certainty of its knowledge about the world, for its satisfaction about what it had accomplished, for its happiness, but the root of the problem was Christianity. For the last two thousand years, he argued, Western civilization had been humiliated by a God that had made sinners out of men and women. The New Testament morality of good and evil had stunted human beings by turning weakness into a virtue. The only way that human beings could recover their full potential and realize their strengths, according to Nietzsche, was to reject God and the stifling moralities imposed in his name. This argument was very offensive to many readers. But it is the key to Nietzsche's thought because he truly believed that it was humans who created all moral systems, who invented supernatural powers and deities, and who therefore could get rid of God as easily as they had made him up. This conviction led Nietzsche to an even more radical proposition, which was that concepts, theories, and beliefs were simply imaginative descriptions of the world. There was no real world beyond our creative rendering of it. Nietzsche believed this insight to be extraordinarily liberating because it meant that humanity was not headed toward one single authoritative or true comprehension of reality but could create and live in endlessly different realities. And just as this insight had fashioned Christianity in one audacious step two thousand years ago, it could invent something else with another step. What Nietzsche called his "perspectivism" corresponds to the relativism of postmodernism today, which puts forward the idea that the way we interact with the world depends on how we describe it. Twentieth-century philosophy is very much the product of and a response to Nietzsche's radical perspectivism and his defiant immoralism. His contention that there is no world outside the interpretations we produce of it continues to attract, astonish, and anger readers.

Nietzsche famously announced that "God is dead" but he also wanted to reanimate the gods. Nietzsche firmly rejected Christian ideas about the divine and the afterlife, and he despised the concept of sin. That is why he spoke about moving "beyond good and evil." Nonetheless, Nietzsche did retain enough piety to be offended by the typical atheists who surrounded him. His "godless theology" was paradoxical because it acknowledged the death of God while denying that death to be a confirmation of the rational, secular, and scientific worldview.[5] For this reason, Nietzsche wrote completely outside modernity; he did not feel authorized by the accumulated wisdom of the Enlightenment as did almost all the leading thinkers of his age. To truly understand the death of God, Nietzsche insisted, atheists would have to appreciate the role that the birth of God had played in the past and the role that the birth of new gods might play in the future. Nietzsche did not believe in God, but he did believe that the audacity of belief was what made human beings fully human.

Nietzsche enticed readers because he described the world in an utterly new way. He used words in order to jolt readers, to dynamite them out of their preconceptions. Precisely because Nietzsche believed that language was a series of common expressions that inhibited creative thought, he experimented with shocking ways of saying things. His hyperbole, in which people kill God, supermen are cruel, ears are enormous, truth is error, are all designed to knock readers off the feet of their assumptions; he admits he "philosophizes with a hammer."[6] With his paradoxes he is constantly "in your face." (It should be added that Nietzsche is most offensive when he makes dumb racist and misogynist assertions.) The fairy-tale parables that Nietzsche tells, especially in *Thus Spoke Zarathustra* (1883–1885), his most popular, accessible book, seem to come from a completely different era. Moreover, his images and metaphors restlessly change, shifting vantage points and flanks of attack. Sometimes Nietzsche prefers to think with mountains, altitudes, and stairs; elsewhere he is in the desert with camels or he is dancing around statues. He rewrites the Bible against itself with references to tablets, which his heroes shatter, or the Crucifixion, which he believes is the fate that the murderers of God endure. Among his favorite images are eyes, which blink or remain awake and see and resee the world anew. This emphasis on eyes is in keeping with Nietzsche's conviction that human beings can interact only with the world they have described and that they move on to new experiences by redescribing the world. His poetic and figurative uses of language all signal the fabricated, changeable, and fundamentally unstable nature of meaning.

With things so protean, Nietzsche never formulated a systematic philosophy, which invited readers to jump into his texts and sometimes allowed them to flounder. For the most part, he wrote in small chunks. The fragments that make up *Thus Spoke Zarathustra* are rarely longer than five or six paragraphs; *The Gay Science* (1882), *Beyond Good and Evil* (1886), and *On the Genealogy of Morals* (1887) are also composed in discrete numbered or named sections. It is the short aphorism, the lightly written paradox or witty insight, that is most typical of Nietzsche's texts. He wrote a total of 2,650 aphorisms, a signal that this line of inquiry was central to his philosophy.[7] Although they are sometimes enigmatic, as Nietzsche admitted, aphorisms do not correspond to a fixed system of meaning; they are open-ended, incomplete, and thus alive to energetic, active readers.[8] For example, Nietzsche writes the following aphorism, whose title is "Enemies of truth": "Convictions are more dangerous enemies of truth than lies" (Document 1). This contains the seeds of Nietzsche's entire theory of knowledge in which truths are simply convictions and lies are the leftovers of obsolescent or defeated arguments. He does not argue the point out, but lets the aphorism slowly twist in the wind. Both Nietzsche's style and his content remind readers that things are not as they seem, or that things are as they are simply because we have made them so.

NIETZSCHE'S IDEAS

The audacious declaration that "God is dead" is an effective way to get at Nietzsche's condemnation of Christian morality and modern democracy, his perspectival theory of knowledge, and finally his quest for new mythical ways of living. These are the common themes in Nietzsche's writings over the entire span of his life. The role of the gods is a central motif in all of Nietzsche's books, from *The Birth of Tragedy* (1872), to the highly personal *Thus Spoke Zarathustra* (1883), his most well-known text, through the powerful syntheses *Beyond Good and Evil* (1886) and *On the Genealogy of Morals* (1887), and finally to his last autobiographical fragments in *Ecce Homo* (1889). Nietzsche's announcement of the death of God was first detonated in *The Gay Science*, which he published in a small edition in 1882. Let's look at the explosive device.

"God Is Dead"

What does it mean for Nietzsche to say, "God is dead"? The proposition is first introduced in the parable "The madman" in *The Gay Science*, and it surprises readers because it is different from the more familiar insistence "There is no God." "God is dead" implies that God was once alive. Moreover, it is a madman whom Nietzsche chooses to send into the marketplace and cry out the question "Where has God gone?" and then answer his own question with *"We have killed him. You and I!"*[9] (see Document 5, section 125). And Nietzsche has the people collected at the marketplace stare back at the madman "in astonishment," suggesting that he has "come too early" only to be misunderstood. But the madman turns away, not so much because the people still believe in God whereas he does not; Nietzsche actually describes the onlookers as nonbelievers. What the people do not understand is what it means to be the murderer of God. The people who have murdered him do not know they have done so or realize that they hold in their hands the bloody knives that have killed him. It is the admission of the murder of God rather than the concession of the fact of the death of God that the madman proclaims. Nietzsche makes the scene gory in order to expose the murderers, not the victim; the momentous act of killing, not the mute result of a dead God. He wants readers to see themselves as murderers because such a recognition would enable them to see themselves as a people who can make and destroy God and thus a people who are strong and creative and have taken control of every aspect of their lives. Nietzsche's madman urges the crowd in the marketplace to live in the open, with the full knowledge of its strengths. If this were possible, the acknowledged murderers of God would surely appear to themselves as God-like. In one of the many paradoxes in Nietzsche's thought, the death of God is transformed into the potential rebirth of gods, the murderers into life-givers.

Rephrasing the announcement that "God is dead" into "we have killed him" means that the question is not about what is or is not in the universe (God), but how we see ourselves (whether or not we are up to recognizing ourselves as murderers). This is an important point, because Nietzsche does not want to make verifiable or binding statements about the world. Instead, he wants to explore how the world changes when we think about it in a different manner. The presence of a God who is now dead, who was alive before, and who might live again indicates that, for Nietzsche, nothing exists outside the human imagination. There is no otherworldly or metaphysical realm based on theology. The world is knowable and experienced only through our thoughts and sensations. While this materialist doctrine may seem to have left the world we know spiritually empty, for Nietzsche it expanded the world, which has many things, including God and the death of God. Indeed, it was precisely the certainties about God and about the prohibitive moralities that belief in God so often demanded that abridged experience of the world, so for Nietzsche the death of God is always a gain, not a loss. "God is dead" thus leads Nietzsche to a dramatic theory of knowledge, which can be put in shorthand as "perspectivism." What Nietzsche referred to as the "perspective optics of life" does not make claims about truth; it exposes new and richer ways of thinking about the world based on looking at things in a different manner.

Nietzsche had nothing but scorn for the type of atheist who took the growing disbelief in God to be an unveiling of the "real" material world and thus lived on as if God had never existed. Rather, Nietzsche wants to shake contemporaries out of complacency so that they would see the knives in their hands and know that they had given form and meaning to the world. The death of God is not the realization of living in a God-less world, but a call to take a more active part in this world.

What makes the death of God so dangerous in this rational, secular age is that the moment of self-discovery will slip away if people in the marketplace regard themselves as atheists, rather than as murderers; see only the march of science rather than their ability to create and destroy gods; and thus do not live up to their potential in a God-less universe and end up possessing less than they did in a pious one. What Nietzsche often refers to as "decadence" is knowing about the death of God without knowing oneself as the murderer of God.

Nietzsche is convinced that "this deed," the murder of God, belongs to "a history greater than any history up to now" (see Document 5, section 125) because people are at a crossroads, either recognizing themselves as the murderers of God and living life ever more fully by making new creations, or regarding themselves as atheists and accepting the horizon of the present. Either they move, or stand still. Man is a pretty clever animal, Nietzsche acknowledges. "*His* strength and cleverness [. . .] *broke open* the cage" in the first place, but maybe he is only strong and clever like "a fox who loses his way and goes astray back into his cage," that is, back into a familiar world.[10] Nietzsche has confidence in the strengths that have brought human beings to the crossroads; he knows that more and more people in the marketplace think critically and no longer believe in God. But he is also deeply disappointed that so few have accepted their role as murderers of God or see the messenger in the marketplace as anything but a madman. Nietzsche believes that each person can see the knife in her hand, which makes his philosophy unmistakably affirmative of human possibility; he also fears that most people will not make the effort to catch even the least glimpse of the knife, and this suspicion makes his philosophy unbearably contemptuous of the "herd." For Nietzsche, the death of God poses the question of the limits of atheism, rationalism, and science, which assert that the true world has been discovered and cannot imagine alternatives to it.

Nietzsche depicts the modern dilemma as both these things: the strength to break the cage and the weakness to be led back into it. As to strength, Nietzsche is not overly generous to humankind. He concedes that after a long period of credulity man has become "a mistrustful animal," and that skepticism of the supernatural is related to the rise of the scientific spirit.[11] Still, this mistrust has come "very late" and is offset by the countervailing tendency in human beings to seek faith and certainty. Nietzsche shows the widespread loss of faith in God to be old news, something only the solitary saint in the forest has not heard, precisely so that he can demonstrate that not even the well-known "death of God" has fundamentally diminished "the desire for certainty" or the prevalence of Christian morality, with the result that the liberating effect of God's demise has not been realized. The inability to dare to take the final step, and to regard life not as fixed but as created and changeable, Nietzsche disapprovingly compares to blinking—blinking in the stare of the ultimate challenge.

When people blink, what do they keep in view, and what do they not see? For those who believe that God is dead and science has triumphed, the present is experienced as a zenith in humankind's ability to know the world. "They are clever and know everything that has happened," and as a result people can rest; "they have their little pleasures by day and their little pleasures by night," scoffs Zarathustra—Zarathustra, Nietzsche's favorite among all the figures he made up, part wise man, part madman, Nietzsche's alter ego (see Document 6, "Prologue," section 5). Because they have "discovered happiness," nineteenth-century Europeans embody the "last man," the being who has finally arrived and does not feel any need to continue the journey. In this sense, the death of God becomes nothing more than the vindication of the present moment, which "knows everything" and happily relies on the principles of science and the self-satisfied morality of the golden mean. For Nietzsche it is a pathetic paradox that the death of God has been accompanied by the renewed triumph of Christian morality in the modern forms of democracy and social welfare. Again and again, he furiously condemns the desire for comfort and preservation, the stillness of the lamb that he contrasts to the restlessness of the lion. In this view, modernity is the faith of the fathers and the grandfathers, that is, the philosophers of the Enlightenment in the eighteenth century and the theorists of utilitarianism and liberalism in the nineteenth century, made permanent. There are no longer admissible mysteries and terrors, with the result that "the earth has become small." And "on it hops the last man" (see Document 6, "Prologue," section 5). Believing the present to be the culmination of the past, men and women have "blinked," Nietzsche writes. They have taken what is to be the best or at least to be good enough and no longer ask questions.

There are also Europeans for whom the death of God is more complicated than the triumph of the Enlightenment. They actually feel the emptiness of a world without God. To them, Nietzsche writes, the "sun seems to have just set [. . .] our old world must look more like evening" (see Document 5, section 343). They understand the radical moment presented by the death of God and perhaps even follow Nietzsche's temperamental inclination against the self-satisfactions of the modern age. But their outlook is passive because they do not recognize themselves to be the murderers of God, they are overwhelmed by the meaninglessness of the world and are nihilistic in many ways as a result, and they are therefore unable to take up a new life. They too have blinked. Where the contented see a zenith, the doomsayers see a nadir, but both are paralyzed by the force of events that have preceded them. They are reactive and inclined to look backward, whether in self-satisfaction or in shock.

Nietzsche's "new philosophers," an unnamed cohort of critical thinkers more wished for than accounted for, accept themselves to be the murderers of God, standing in contrast to both the last men, who see the contemporary secular world at its zenith, and the nauseated nihilists, who view the death of God as the end of all belief and purpose. They are "free spirits," like the imaginary Zarathustra, who have taken the next step and freed themselves both from the Christian morality that had accompanied belief in God and the overconfidence of the rational, scientific worldview. Nietzsche's hyperbolic description of murderers and knives is a drastic way of calling attention to life's "plastic powers" (see Document 3), the almost physical capacity to tear into and break with the customs of parents and to sculpt and invent alternate lifeways for the children. "In my children," Nietzsche says, "I want to make up for being the child of my fathers."[12] Far from being a dark, evening event, then, the death of God is "daybreak,"[13] a "new dawn,"[14] and a "new morning."[15] "At long last our ships can set out again to face any danger. All the risks of seeking knowledge are once again permissible. The sea, *our* sea, is once again open; perhaps there was never such an 'open sea'" (see Document 5, section 343). "There are a thousand paths that have never yet been trodden," Nietzsche reiterates in *Thus Spoke Zarathustra*, "a thousand healths and hidden isles of life." "Man's earth" is still "undiscovered."[16] Nietzsche is never clear about what sort of destinations these new "isles of life" are, and because he repeatedly emphasizes that there are thousands of isles to be seen, thousands of paths to be taken, and thousands of houses to be built, it would not really make sense to do so. Rather, his stress is on the journey, leaving home, taking up anchor, and setting out for the open sea. He emphasizes the act of exploration, rather than the arrival of the explorer, the verbs rather than the objects.

The ability to set out on a journey is premised on knowing that it is possible to leave home. This sounds simple, but it means realizing that the laws and customs of home are not binding and that the gods of home are not almighty. How is it that the free spirits come to make these assumptions? Here, as a lover of knowledge, Nietzsche shows himself to stand very much in the Enlightenment tradition. He does not want to get at *the* truth, but to excavate the origins of the many truths that men and women hold dear. This is where the scientific method, if taken seriously, is indispensable. Whereas ordinary people, in Nietzsche's view, take the values of their societies as natural, unquestionable forms, the new philosophers that he invokes regard them as plausible but never necessary judgments on and interpretations of the world. And whereas most of Nietzsche's nineteenth-century contemporaries did not recognize the historical origins of their culture, the new philosophers deployed a historical method to reveal the circumstantial origins of all cultural values and moral perspectives. The rabble, Nietzsche explains, "thinks back all the way to his grandfather—and with his grandfather, time stops. Thus, everything in the past has been abandoned" (see Document 6, "On Old and New Tablets," section 11). By contrast, Nietzsche's Zarathustra and the followers Nietzsche imagines around him recover the past and discover multiple origins and, beyond those origins, previous epochs. They see the flow of time into the present in terms of grand ruptures and new beginnings.

Only the self-professed murderers of a divine God can see that they have created the essential categories of faith and morality and thus can see the historical origins of human culture and respect the variety of ways it has developed. Having seen "many lands and many peoples," Zarathustra explains that "every people speaks its tongue of good and evil" and has "invented its own language of customs and rights."[17] There are many ways of speaking and inventing, but how do these come about and how do they become authoritative so that we can speak about this culture or that culture? Here Nietzsche follows up his rambling travelogue of Zarathustra's journeys with a more sustained analysis in *Beyond Good and Evil* and *On the Genealogy of Morals* of what elements make a society familiar to its members from the inside and distinctive to strangers looking in from the outside. Once Nietzsche has established that morality is just a matter of culture, he concludes that the customs and values of a society are in the end simply lies; that is, they are non-necessary ways of doing things that over time have come to be accepted as truths and even cherished as sacred. He then takes one more step to classify societies as more or less dogmatic, depending on the actions of exceptional individuals that cultures are willing to tolerate, on the degree to which they acknowledge themselves to be living a lie, and on the extent to which rules and regulations have become rigid and lifeless. These distinctions enable Nietzsche to launch a critique of Western Christianity, which, in Nietzsche's view, has become inflexible and degenerate. But his critique of the contemporary world rests on his analysis of the social origins of morality as such, and this must be examined first.

Society, Language, and Truth

Nietzsche was very much a child of his age. He was aware of the prehistoric depth of human history with discoveries such as the bones of prehistoric hominids in the Neander Valley of western Germany in 1856. Given his fascination with imaginary journeys to "hidden isles," Nietzsche was also keenly aware of the ethnographic variation that European explorers around the globe had brought to light in the eighteenth century and that spurred the first generation of anthropologists in his own time to speculate on the origins of human society. Finally, Nietzsche incorporated important ideas about trial and error in the process of human evolution, as suggested by Charles Darwin (*The Origin of Species* [1859]). However, where most scientists saw evolution as progression, Nietzsche simply saw ceaseless transformation without any necessary direction: After all, "we have invented the concept of 'end.'"[18]

In Nietzsche's view, what separates humans from other animals is collective life in a society in which members must communicate to survive. "As the most endangered animal," Nietzsche concludes, "man *needed* help, shelter, and his own kind" and "he needed to know how to express his distress and make himself understood" (see Document 5, section 354). In order to express themselves, humans developed common languages, and these languages in turn provided humans with the tools by which they could explore and know themselves. Without language there is no knowledge, and as a result, men and women knew themselves only through the words, images, and concepts with which they named their feelings and described the world around them. It was as a "social animal" that man first became "conscious of himself" and developed a language to convey that consciousness. Thus "our thoughts" about our innermost selves "are continually [. . .] translated back into the perspective of the herd" (see Document

5, section 354). To get at Nietzsche's meaning, it is useful to think about "common sense"; the phrase designates knowledge about the world held in common and thus leads to predictable behavior that, in turns, verifies the designation of "common sense" to actions and reactions. Ultimately, language allowed speakers to reflect on the possession of language itself and on the way that language created and strengthened social modes of being. As a result, it could accommodate interpretive variations to one or another degree. Nonetheless, individuals had to use the social products of a common language to relate to others and to think about themselves. "The *you* is older than the *I*,"[19] Nietzsche insists. Social forms, common language, and collective morality always came first, the idea of the individual only afterward.

Around the world, human beings formed many different groups and developed very different kinds of conceptual toolboxes as they adapted to the environments in which they lived. But over time, groups sought to preserve their identity as distinct; they energetically distinguished themselves from other groups. The cultural values they prized were not so much direct functional responses to life in the mountains or life by the sea, although these environmental distinctions were important, but markers of the particularity and greatness of the group. "Once you have recognized the adversity and land and sky and neighbors of a people," Nietzsche writes about the origins of society, "then you have surely understood the law of its overcomings and the reason it climbs this particular ladder to its aspirations" (see Document 6, "On the Thousand and One Goals"); needs become beliefs. While societies were founded in material necessities—"land and sky"—they developed in history by virtue of their own "overcomings," that is, an internal dynamic that made valuable and sacred the customs they found to be indispensable. These were written into laws, adopted into custom, and thereby constituted cultural tablets no different in their function than that of the Ten Commandments in the Old Testament. Indeed, Nietzsche repeatedly uses the loaded imagery of "tablets" to push readers to see Christianity's beliefs as parts of a historical process of tablet writing that had nothing to do with revelations of God. Groups became "powerful and eternal" by transforming practical environmental adaptations into long-standing cultural identities or myths (see Document 6, "On the Thousand and One Goals"). These became the markers by which insiders knew their culture as sacred and by which outsiders knew it to be different and distinct. The creation of myths thereby established a homogeneous order within society and a system of differences among societies.

The world is not the product of our senses or of our verifiable experience in it, Nietzsche claims, and thus the universe described by the language and concepts of one group cannot be directly translated into what might be called the "word universe" of another. There is no common or real world "out there" because there is always the irreducible presence of different cultures and languages that enables unique interpretations. According to Nietzsche, everything that humans experience is comprehended and passed on in terms of the distinct vocabularies that the groups they belong to have fashioned. "So, what, then, is truth?" Nietzsche asks. "It is a mobile army of metaphors, metonyms, and anthropomorphisms—in short, a sum of human relations, which have been enhanced, transposed, and embellished in poetry and rhetoric" (see Document 2). (A good example of a metaphor is the way the word *instinct* is used following this passage in Document 2.) This means that there is no world aside from interpretations of it. Moreover, if everything is a matter of perspective, it follows that actions cannot be intrinsically good or bad: "there are no moral phenomena, only a moral interpretation of phenomena" (see Document 1). Nietzsche repeatedly insists that it is human beings, driven by the needs of socialization, who have imposed meaning onto countless contexts.

Nietzsche is dazzled by these audacious acts of creation. Precisely because social groups did not read the world around them in a verifiable way or in terms of the cognitive structure of the human mind, as the eighteenth-century philosopher Immanuel Kant had suggested, but knew the world only in terms of the words and concepts they had fashioned, they exercised a naive mastery over their own totally personal cosmos. "The charm of the Platonic way of thinking," Nietzsche writes about the ancient Greeks he loved so dearly, was that it "consisted precisely in *resistance* to obvious sense-evidence" and "this by means of pale, cold, gray concept nets which they threw over the motley whirl of the senses."[20] The Greeks pictured the world through stories in which men and women played active, powerful parts. Every society in its own way turned experience into myth and perception into faith.

There is no doubt that the "army of metaphors," which suggests that a society is like a beehive, perhaps, or the brain like a computer, always mobilizes an erroneous picture of the world. Here Nietzsche uses modern scientific or analytic methods in order to expose the untruthful quality of knowledge. There is a basic error in the foundation of all cultural systems and it is the result of the very act of naming things. We think that we speak very precisely, but actually Nietzsche maintains that we speak in a very generic way. The exactness of a word, for example, slips into the general embrace of a concept, Nietzsche explains, "inasmuch as it is *not* intended to serve as a reminder of the unique and wholly individual original experience to which it owes its origin, but rather must fit countless more or less similar cases." Otherwise, communication would be impossible. "Every concept is generated," he continues, by "equating unequal things." At this point, Nietzsche pauses to give an example: "Since no leaf is totally the same as another, the concept 'leaf' is formed by arbitrarily discarding the individual differences among leaves and by forgetting the distinguishing aspects" (see Document 2). Naming involves remembering commonalities, which remain present in one form or another, but every collective noun (*leaves*) also involves forgetting the differences between things, which are deleted. Nietzsche sometimes holds out the possibility that a group might retain, at least for a time, the distinction between the thing and what it is named, know that "leaf" cannot possibly suggest all "leaves," and can more or less consciously live with the metaphors and myths it has fashioned. But the tendency is for metaphors to become certainties, and particular ways of doing things to become rules. "After long use," Nietzsche argues, the metaphors "seem fixed, canonical, and binding to a people. Truths are illusions that we have forgotten are illusions." In this case, the truth is the widespread use of "customary metaphors," the reflex or obligation "to lie according to established conventions, to lie collectively in a manner binding for everyone" (see Document 2). Study of the linguistic nature of interaction with the world exposes the basic paradox that "truth" rests on error and life in groups consists of living in error.

Any number of thinkers in the Enlightenment tradition followed Nietzsche's historical or genealogical method this far. They stopped there, however, satisfied that the science of history and the study of language had proven preexisting ("premodern") systems of knowledge to be false. They were content to regard the present state of ("modern") Western knowledge as superior in its clarifications. However, this satisfaction in modern scholarship Nietzsche found totally arid because it did not provide meaning to the world. "Any custom is better than no custom," wrote Nietzsche, expressing his disdain for nineteenth-century thinkers who gleefully emptied the buckets of past tradition without filling up their own.[21] However erroneous, the acts of making the world appear familiar, sacred, or divine are just what make human beings so "interesting" and different from other animals (see

Document 8, First Essay, section 6). To understand the historical origins of morality does not provide any conclusions about the value of this or that morality. This last question is the real one Nietzsche wants to pose, and in his historical analysis of "the genealogy of morals" he wants to finish up the historical parts of his interpretation so that he can get to the judgmental parts and particularly to his critique of Western Christianity. But he needs to take one more step.

If the basic paradox is that truth rests in error (because any way of life is simply the distorting sight line of metaphor that might say "I am a work in progress" or "I am God's creation" or "I am my genes"), the paradox that follows is that error is a sign of life.[22] Nietzsche repeatedly distinguishes humans from other animals because they have created a vocabulary of names and a system of signs, that is, myths or stories to live by. This queer, strange world is what we admire in the ancient Greeks and it is why we are drawn to them. But the richness or, as Nietzsche would put it, the "profundity" of any worldview lies in the particular kind of error or, we might say, interpretation, on which that worldview is premised. Not to be in error is not to have a way of looking at the world and thus not to be a social being. Nietzsche provides the paradoxical conclusion that "every profound spirit needs a mask," one that is a "consistently false, namely, *shallow* interpretation to each of his words, each of his steps, each sign of his life" that the spirit gives (see Document 7, section 40). The collective act of cultural creation reveals the "will to appearances, to simplification, to masks, to cloaks, in short, to surface" (see Document 7, section 230) because collective identity demands a common language and thus the maintenance of the culture's kind of error. Every culture possesses its own illusion of the truth. In the end, Nietzsche insists that the preservation of culture depends on a kind of acquired naiveté that is willing to celebrate error as its fancy.

Nietzsche repeatedly uses hyperbolic vocabulary that contrasts truth with error, and profundity with simplification, because he wants to shake readers out of their "commonsense" assumption that there is one knowable reality "out there" and to push them to see that culture and knowledge are imaginative interpretations of the world. Every interpretation is a simplification because it reduces the huge abundance of things in the world to nameable and knowable concepts. And it is precisely this translation of things into forces that allows humans to interact with the world: "How we have made everything around us clear and free and easy and simple! how we have been able to give our senses a passport to everything superficial," and "how from the beginning we have contrived to retain our ignorance in order to enjoy an almost inconceivable freedom, lack of scruple and caution, heartiness, and gaiety of life."[23] In yet another paradox, Nietzsche claims that only this ability to enjoy and master the world we have named makes possible the eventual freedom to explore illusions, lies, and untruth. Without the practice of playing in the garden of our own fairy tale, then, it would not be possible to break with the fairies and tell a new tale.

Nietzsche is fully aware that men and women who question the basic premises of their own culture or offer alternative vocabularies will be mocked. They are like the murderers of gods; with their passions "the self-confidence of the community collapses, its faith in itself" (see Document 7, section 201). The necessity to preserve the myth that gives the group its identity will not tolerate the "non-adorer who dwells in the woods."[24] A person who breaks tablets is branded a "law-breaker" and designated as evil. In world history, it is the murderers of gods who have been crucified, Nietzsche concludes in another audacious paradox (see Document 6, "On the Way of the Creator" and "On Old and New Tablets"). Yet societies also differ in the extent to which they tolerate "non-adorers" and critics like Nietzsche. It is at this point that Nietzsche feels he is finally authorized to assess moral systems.

Good and Bad versus Good and Evil

To make apparent how cultures deal with different and new ways of looking at the world, and to be able to get a handle on the spiritual impoverishment of the present day, Nietzsche distinguishes between two systems of morality, one characterized by the distinction between good and bad, which Nietzsche identifies with the Greeks and other ancient cultures, and the other characterized by the distinction between good and evil, for which Western Christianity and nineteenth-century Europe are the primary examples. That the second system succeeded the first is one of those audacious examples of creative transformation, something Nietzsche cherishes in a formal way. But this particular succession Nietzsche never ceases to condemn as a crime against the potentialities of men and women because it has produced what he calls the dominant "slave morality" of the West in which people see each other as victims instead of as masters of their own lives.

The distinction between good and bad, on the one hand, and good and evil, on the other, is central to Nietzsche's thought, and it is the only way he differentiates among the countless acts of cultural creation that make up the history of humankind. In his analysis, Nietzsche puts the succession from an older, more heroic to a newer, diminished worldview front and center. He puts aside his insights into the extraordinary variety of moral systems to concentrate on just two in order to emphasize the world historical moment of the birth of Judeo-Christian morality some two thousand years ago and to emphasize as well the opportunity available in the present day to abandon it. At times, Nietzsche suggests that Western Christianity has triumphed in an enormous but contemptible transformation of moral values. At other times, Nietzsche choreographs the conflict between good and bad *and* good and evil as a relentless battle that takes place at the very heart of European society and in each and every individual. But his overall purpose remains the same: to make understandable the historical moment when Christianity began to exert its crushing moral power, to demonstrate the persistence of Christianity's slave morality in today's secular age in the form of democracy, and to embolden the murderers of God to acknowledge their act of deicide in order to demolish not only God but the slave morality in which the power of God continues to persist.

In the ancient morality of good and bad, what is good is what distinguishes humans from other animals: their ability to name the universe and their desire to play in the universe they have created. Anything that expands the powers of men and women to feel masterful is good. "What is good?" Nietzsche asks. "Everything that heightens the feeling of power in man."[25] By contrast, what is bad are those things that keep people from creating and recreating the sense of mastery, that is to say, everything that is ordinary, satisfied, and comfortable. What this distinction implies is that good and bad are not judgments on the intentions of protagonists but judgments on how well the actions of protagonists have enhanced what it might mean to be human. Good may well embrace dangerous and lustful drives. Here is an example of what Nietzsche means by good and bad in the realm of sexual politics: People would not be good because they have remained loyal to a husband or wife, but because they acted on their amorous passions whether or not infidelity was the consequence. Nietzsche is not saying you *should* be unfaithful to your lover, but rather be faithful to yourself if you *want* to take another lover. Such actions would be life-enhancing even when they are hurtful and self-indulgent. In the end, the avoidance of cruelty is too high a price to pay not to explore different kinds of love.[26] What Nietzsche cherished was accomplishment and experimentation, which meant acquiring new identities, leaving behind the customs of fathers and grandfathers, and testing out new descriptions of the world.

Nietzsche often used military vocabulary that suggested his acceptance or encouragement of war in the making of a strong society, whose dangerous and brave warriors would in turn spur further accomplishments. Noble creative actions might well mean killing the enemy or, as in the example of love and lovers, abandoning husbands or wives. Nietzsche would not have rejected these ways of enhancing collective or individual life. But his emphasis on cruelty is misunderstood if readers dwell simply on the actual indulgence in physical or emotional pain. By cruelty Nietzsche means the willingness to break the tablets of law and order and shatter cherished assumptions, even your own, what in *Zarathustra* he refers to "the risky adventure," "the cruel No" (see Document 6, "On Old and New Tablets," section 7).

In the ancient world of good and bad, god's role was life-enhancing: "a god who helps, who devises means, who is at bottom the word for every happy inspiration of courage and self-confidence."[27] What Nietzsche has in mind when he writes these lines is the family of gods in ancient Greece, where myths enabled men and women to act in all the ways that made them fully human. Greece was cherished by nineteenth-century Europeans as the cradle of civilization, for the philosophy and science it bequeathed to Europe, but Nietzsche loved it in a different manner. He revered exactly what distinguished Greece from the overarching authority of the Christianity that followed: the sheer variety of Greek cultural traditions in Athens, Sparta, and elsewhere; the scale of emotional registers in Greek comedy and tragedy; and the polytheistic, many-sided relations that the Greeks maintained with their gods. By inventing many gods, some who celebrated exuberant passion, such as Dionysius, and others who honored self-discipline, such as Apollo, the Greeks developed *any number of norms* and broke with the formative systems of morality that Nietzsche had analyzed in his historical surveys. In the prehistoric era, it was true that "there was only one norm," and opposition to holding "ideals of one's own" was the "foundation of all custom." What was new about the innovative polytheism of the Greeks was that it made possible the unprecedented "luxury" of becoming an individual. In this important section in *The Gay Science* (see Document 5, section 143), Nietzsche explains that a universe inhabited by "gods, heroes, and supermen of all kinds, as well as near-men and submen, dwarfs, fairies, centaurs, satyrs, demons, and devils, was the priceless first attempt to vindicate the selfhood and self-love of the individual." What he means is that this varied company invited all sorts of ways of interacting with divine creatures and eventually gave men and women the possibility to create for themselves the ideals and freedom to determine their own "laws, customs, and neighbors." "Polytheism provided an example for the freespiritedness and many-spiritedness of humanity; the strength to create for ourselves our own new eyes—and ever again new eyes that are even more our own: hence man alone among all the animals has no eternal horizons or perspectives" (Document 5, section 143). This wonderful sentence is a clear statement of what makes people distinctively human: the will to see things with new eyes and from fresh perspectives. Nietzsche believed that Greek culture facilitated this; Christianity did not.

People might do stupid things, as the gods frequently pointed out in the myths that the Greeks handed down (see Document 8, Second Essay, section 25), but mortals were not condemned as sinners precisely because their desire for mastery and their feelings of lust were the very things that differentiated them from animals. Nietzsche's world of good and bad was not necessarily pretty or peaceful, but it was a place that nourished vigorous forms of life. Of course, Nietzsche added in an aside, "we are quite justified in continuing to fear" those strong, dangerous individuals who break tablets, but, he asks, "what man would not a hundred times sooner be terrified, but also admire, than *not* be terrified at all, but never be rid of the nauseating sight of what is misshapen, shriveled, wasted, and poisoned?" (see Document 8, First Essay, section 11). While no culture can allow strong individuals to do as they like, the ancient Greeks and the early Romans, with their morality of good and bad, showed them remarkable leniency.

The morality of good and evil developed in opposition to the morality of good and bad. Good and evil were the designations of a universal moral system in which the virtuous intentions of the actor and the benefits to the group as a whole were central, whereas good and bad referred exclusively to what did or did not serve the vital forces of life. Nietzsche's account of the origins of what he calls the "revaluation of values" gives a better sense of the distinction between the two conceptions of morality (see Document 7, section 203). Nietzsche gives a variety of reasons for this transformation. Sometimes, it is the defeat and enslavement of the Jews that forced a once joyous, free people to submit to the stern demands of their God in order to survive as a group. Elsewhere, Nietzsche blames the class of priests who created the doctrine of sin and described God's rewards and punishments in order to hold onto power as divine mediators, although this seems to be more an aggravating than an original cause. For the main part, Nietzsche blames the resentment that ordinary people felt for the accomplishments of strong free spirits. Resentment, or the French *ressentiment*, is a word that Nietzsche uses over and over again and it instructs the reader to see resentment, revenge, and envy as the principal hinges in the audacious moral revaluation of good and bad into good and evil.

"It was the refined races who left behind them the concept 'barbarian' wherever they went," writes Nietzsche in *On the Genealogy of Morals*. At first glance, readers might imagine Nietzsche to mean that refined men distinguished themselves from barbarians just as they distinguished good from bad. But what Nietzsche means is that "their shocking cheerfulness and their profound delight in all destruction and in the cruel liberties of victory," which he identifies with human creativity and is the "good" part of good and bad, was regarded as barbaric by "those who suffered from it" (see Document 8, First Essay, section 11). It was the victims who began to refer to the refined races as the barbaric "evil enemies" and assigned moral judgment to their harmful actions. This is how the lesser Greek city-states regarded the Athenians, the Jews the Romans, and sedentary Europeans the Germanic Goths. Even within a society, the weak, the sick, and the meek—the ordinary mass of people whom Nietzsche sometimes refers to as the herd, or as slaves because they do not live the ideal of masterful existence—resent the strong and creative. In Nietzsche's view, they came to define themselves as victims, in terms of what they did not have and were thus resentful. Whereas good and bad were terms used by actors to designate what did or did not further accomplishment, good and evil were designated by the victims, so that "evil" was whatever made people suffer and "good" was the quality of suffering virtuously.

In the morality of good and evil, the weak are not actually weaker and the strong not actually stronger. At one point, Nietzsche honors the free spirit, the strong man in the morality of good and bad, who does not take his enemies, accidents, or misdeeds "seriously for very long"—he acknowledges that bad things happen to good people (see Document 8, First Essay, section 10). The difference between the strong and the weak is not strength, but what individuals make of their imperfections; the strong (in a morality of good and bad) continue to strive and will possibly fail. However, when the weak fail (in a morality of good and evil), they blame outside forces and indulge their incapacities. Again, for Nietzsche, it is a matter of perception rather than ability.

In a fascinating parable, Nietzsche strolls alongside Zarathustra "over the great bridge" where at once "cripples and beggars surrounded him" (see Document 6, "On Redemption"). A hunchback offers Zarathustra the opportunity to "heal the blind and make the lame walk" and to take away from those who have "too much" and return a small bit to those who have less. But Zarathustra refuses to do so; he has neither sympathy for the hunchback nor desire to redistribute the fortunes and misfortunes of life. He rejects pity because he believes that the victims have become what he calls "inverse cripples." In explanation, Zarathustra tells about his encounters with sufferers who identify themselves completely with what they do not have. Rather than remain men, they have become the leg that is broken, the eye that no longer sees, the belly that is not filled. Nietzsche is rather cruel (and funny) in the way he makes his point: "when I [. . .] crossed this bridge for the first time, I could not believe my eyes and looked again and again." What he saw was "an ear as big as a man." "Attached to this enormous ear was a small slender stalk," legs, trunk, and arms. "With a magnifying glass you could even make out a tiny envious face." Such a creature is the horrible product of the morality of pity. Across the world, Zarathustra reports, he has walked "among men as among the fragments and limbs of men." He sees "fragments and limbs and dreadful accidents — but no human beings." For Nietzsche, the cripples and beggars who speak to Zarathustra only in terms of what they do not have and of what Zarathustra might give back to them are little more than the body pieces they lack. They see themselves only in the magnified reflection of their debility and thus walk around as giant eyes or enormous ears. This is the physical incarnation of resentment.

The revaluation of good and bad into good and evil is accomplished when cripples and beggars see themselves as legs and bellies and convince society to make up the losses they have suffered. What Nietzsche describes as the morality of the "sickroom" is sustained by the resentment of the have-nots and is designed to compensate them in an act of revenge against the haves.[28] It is very important to remember that Nietzsche is not separating out the weak from the strong or the poor from the rich, or celebrating the fortunate; he knows that heroes suffer. Rather, he is condemning the centrality that suffering plays in ideas about the meaning of life. In a morality of resentment, good is what relieves pain and injustice, and evil is what is indifferent to or aggravates pain. In a world that cultivates pity, "all freedom, all pride, all self-confidence of the spirit" are stifled, inequalities are not tolerated, and "the poor, the powerless, the downtrodden alone are the good" (see Document 8, First Essay, section 7).[29] The victims of the barbarians, the cripples at the great bridge, and the ancient Jews, whose collective identity, in Nietzsche's view, was tied to the experience of suffering at the hands of Roman imperialists — they have all contributed to the revaluation of morality. But it was the early Christians who took the biggest step in codifying the morality of good and evil. It was the Christians and the priestly class they created who sought their influence by, and derived their power from, speaking in the name of the victim.

In *On the Genealogy of Morals*, Nietzsche sets the scene two thousand years ago as early Christians energetically tended to the sick and the poor and set up a vast network of mutual aid societies and charities.[30] In Nietzsche's view, they thereby created a timid, suffering herd that reacted with fear to a "hostile outside world," a herd that formed the basis of Christianity's overwhelming power (see Document 8, First Essay, section 10). While Christians could not actually undo or redistribute the misfortunes of life, they created a morality that valorized the meek and powerless and demeaned the strong, who were instructed not to let their free-spiritedness lead them into temptation and error. By inventing the concept of sin, Christianity enabled the weak to take revenge on the strong, whose self-stylized norms were now regarded as contraventions of God's will. No longer enabling life, as had the gods of ancient Greece, the Christian God demanded renunciation, ultimately leading, in Nietzsche's view, to the diminishment of life itself. In other words, Christian morality limited the strong in the same way that lack of will had once limited the weak. It thereby created a common, suffering humanity. It was not only the herd's spirit of revenge that enforced this morality of good and evil. It was also the promise of a glorious afterlife that served to compensate for this lamentable worldly life. Henceforth, the promise of God's rewards justified the acceptance of God's punishments, with a priestly class serving as the accountants to God's moral balance sheets. A single, all-powerful God established a single moral law that was inscribed onto the tablets of monotheism. These laws or commandments strictly regulated behavior with the concept of sin, the activity of consecration, and the threat of casting out naysayers as heretics and apostates. This moral enforcement was the singular achievement of Christianity.

That early Christianity turned hatred, the resentment against the masterful barbarians who made their own laws, into love, in this case for the weak, is one of Nietzsche's favorite paradoxes, and it underscores how extraordinary he considered the transformation of morality. He admits a grudging respect for how Christians turned the tables (or tablets) on the free spirits. He also praises the Jews for their resistance to the older morality of good and bad and for their devotion to the new morality of good and evil. This enabled the Jews to assert their collective identity in the face of hostile enemies—the Assyrians, the Egyptians, and the Romans in ancient times, the Christians in ours—over the course of centuries. But for the fact that the "slave rebellion" of the Jews spread in the Christian era and turned into an authoritative, powerful code of conduct across the Western world, Nietzsche has only the sharpest criticism. Step by step, the slaves reined in the masters with the convictions of sin, and step by step, the masters developed what Nietzsche calls a "bad conscience," which is how the morality of good and evil seeped into the masters and monitored their behavior. Nietzsche provides striking images of the former master with a guilty conscience: "this deprived creature," "this animal . . . rubbing itself raw against the bars of its cage" (see Document 8, Second Essay, section 16). For exceptionally strong individuals—Nietzsche mentions the fourth-century theologian Augustine of Hippo and the Renaissance scholar Blaise Pascal—the struggle to accept Christian morality was protracted. Again and again, they lapsed into Christian sin, that is, into their old freedoms, which Nietzsche captures in the image of "god on the cross" (for it is the strong, not the weak, the vigorous, not the virtuous who are crucified, in Nietzsche's view) before embarking on another cycle of religious renunciation.[31] Only with extraordinary force of will did these sinners master their temptations and thereby provide the herd with celebrated examples of ascetic or saintly existence. In another one of Nietzsche's mischievous paradoxes, it is the Christian holy man who is the closest thing to the free spirit of the ancient world. All that is left of individualism is self-mutilation and self-contempt. For this reason, Nietzsche saw Christianity as the religion that first made humans hate themselves.

But Nietzsche does not let it go at that, and he steps back to survey once more the audacious revaluation of morality. This spectacle of an animal "taking sides against itself," Nietzsche remarks, was "so new, deep, unprecedented, mysterious, contradictory" that it actually confirmed the "great promise" of humankind even if Christianity itself explicitly rejected the notion that its codes and tablets were not eternally valid, but only "an episode, a bridge" to something else. No matter, because it was the very break that Christianity achieved, the world-historical difference it made, that gives Nietzsche confidence in his view of the world as a series of utterly innovative breaks in which men and women create for themselves their "own new eyes." "From now on," he writes in *On the Genealogy of Morals*, there can be no doubt, "man has to be counted *among* the most unexpected and exciting lucky throws in the game of dice played by Heraclitus' 'great child,' be he called Zeus or chance." For all the pessimism with which Nietzsche regards Christianity, it is contained in a more sweeping optimism about the "great promise" of humankind (see Document 8, Second Essay, section 16). This is why Nietzsche wants the murderers of God to acknowledge what they have done—so they will continue to play the game of dice.

The Cocoon of Modernity

Nietzsche is sometimes overwhelmed by the sheer staying power of Christian morality. Masterful individuals occasionally make their appearance in Western history, Cesare Borgia, the most powerful of the Renaissance popes, for example, or Napoleon in the modern era. And Nietzsche lauds the scientific spirit of inquiry, if not the certainty or the meaningfulness it places in the answers it provides, and he grudgingly notes the value the Protestant Reformation gave to the individual interpretation of sacred texts, although not its insistence on humanity's basic sinfulness. But the big picture is the same: The slave morality of resentment remains pervasive in the present day, even as scientists and philosophers claim that they no longer believe in God. Even the Enlightenment is fundamentally misguided because it regards its insights into the natural world, the human mind, and civic life as definitive truths rather than fanciful experiments, as real knowledge, not just different descriptions. Nietzsche simply does not accept the great conceit of modernity, which is its certainty in its advancement over the cultures of the past and its cleverness in understanding nature. It is precisely because modern Europeans were so sure that they were at the zenith of intellectual development that they proved to be completely unwilling to see or imagine themselves with "new eyes." This incomprehension of anything but what *is* constitutes modernity's biggest flaw. With this critique, Nietzsche stands out as one of the few thinkers of the nineteenth century to think outside of the modernity ushered in by the Enlightenment, the French Revolution, and the scientific and industrial revolutions.

The historical event that Nietzsche returns to again and again is the revaluation of morality when Christianity eclipsed Greek and Roman civilization some two thousand years ago. And basically nothing has changed. Since then, however, the enforcement of the slave morality has gradually passed from the priests of monotheism to the administrators of the modern state. After the French Revolution, which Nietzsche describes as "the last great slave rebellion" of the powerless against the powerful, European society increasingly organized its activities around improving conditions for the masses.[32] Parliamentary government, in which more and more ordinary men could vote and seek office, worked with the intention of replacing commanders with "clever herd men," Nietzsche argues, and saw as its function the legislation of what was most useful to the greatest number, "namely, public spirit, good will, respect for others, industriousness [. . .] and empathy."[33] The proclaimed duty of modern government was service to the public, that new nineteenth-century entity that enabled more people to make their way up in the world, acquire an education, find employment, protect their children, and do so on a more or less equal footing. Nietzsche despises the modern state precisely because it destroys the differences inherent in the prerevolutionary estates and corporations, invents its own authoritative and leveling language of "customs and rights," and standardizes knowledge by providing general education for all.[34] Socialists, who sought more than just public access to opportunities, which liberals championed, but also the redistribution of wealth in the name of the less fortunate, were even worse; those "louts and blockheads" wanted nothing less than the "animalization of men turned into stunted little animals with equal rights and equal claims" (see Document 7, section 203). For all the pertinent differences between English utilitarians and German socialists, they came together in their service to the public, valorizing what served it and recommending its political empowerment.

What springs to mind when we read these fulminations is Nietzsche's disgust at the sight of a hospital or a nursery, his contempt for a public meeting or a deliberative body. This is true, but does not get at the main point of Nietzsche's attacks. What Nietzsche does not respect is the person who finds the meaning of life in the diminishment of its difficulties. If conventional life is a "contract," a full life should be an "experiment," announces Zarathustra (see Document 6, "On Old and New Tablets," section 25). Moreover, Nietzsche is uninterested in all the energy that goes into making the public comfortable, when people should be challenged and tested. It is the spiritual effect of social legislation that Nietzsche regards as so paralyzing. Modern men and women have "discovered happiness." The Germans, in particular, are in love with being comfortable and *bieder*, the last a reference to the homey, modest style of the arts in the 1820s and 1830s, and, by extending this cocoon of modernity, they want everybody to be the same (see Document 6, "Prologue," section 5). Of course, people are not exactly the same: The town is motley and the marketplace in its center is colorful. But in their search for happiness and in their contentment with coziness, contemporaries are basically the same. They are the same in their satisfaction at being spectators to lively shows rather than creators of strenuous projects: they gather and gape in the marketplace, at Zarathustra whom they consider a jester or the madman who shouts to the townspeople about the death of God. Modern men and women are the same, Nietzsche continues, because they can see no further than the horizon outlined by their fathers and grandfathers and because they cannot imagine a future fundamentally different from the present they inhabit; they have drowned all the tempests of time in the "shallow waters" of contemporary Europe (see Document 6, "On Old and New Tablets," section 11). It is true that nineteenth-century Europeans honored Nietzsche's beloved Greeks, but they did so without recognizing the restlessness of Greek culture or the plurality of its norms; "Christianity has cheated us out of the harvest of ancient culture," Nietzsche laments.[35] Everything has been officially named, tagged, and designated as a "classic" or condemned as trivial or obsolescent by scholars who are little more than "walking encyclopedias," "thinking-, writing-, and speaking machines" who grind commentary for scholarly canons.[36] (When Nietzsche speaks of slaves, as opposed to masters, he often has these professors in mind.) Sameness is thus an attribute of the physical confinement of creating a cocoon and of the intellectual confinement of regarding the present day as the zenith of all time. It is a function of trusting your eyes, of blinking so as not to create new eyes in order to see the world in new ways.

Superman, or Overman

Nietzsche's contempt for the herd is unmistakable. When the image of the herd is matched with its opposite, the "superman" or *Übermensch* whom Zarathustra heralds on his many journeys up and down the mountains, it is sometimes difficult not to regard Nietzsche as a philosopher of powerful, indifferent, and often violent men. But superman is not characterized by what he does to others, to the weak, but by his strength to constantly change and transform himself, which is why "overman" is a more accurate, although more awkward, translation than is "superman." To be sure, Nietzsche refers to the "blond beast" and he takes the side of barbarians against their victims not just in parables at the "great bridge" but in quite historically specified situations such as the Peloponnesian War waged between the two great ancient Greek city-states, Athens and Sparta, in the fifth century BCE. The ease with which the Nazis appropriated Nietzsche thirty years after his death and placed him in the pantheon of German heroes who validated the division of the world into supermen or "Aryans" and subhumans—that is, Slavs and Jews—suggests that there is indeed a pitiless, even racist aspect to Nietzsche's thought. This is not unwarranted, as Nietzsche's glorification of collective myths reveals. But Nietzsche is truly allergic to the idea of winners; he repeatedly rejects the self-satisfaction of the present day and derides the canonization of Western culture as the "shallow waters" of thought. He is not at ease with the triumphalism of the winner or the zenith of modernity. Although he certainly takes the side of the destructive forces in society, it is not to cheer on incomparable strength; rather, he lauds the resolution to overturn accepted norms, to break the tablets of law, and to redescribe the world in different ways. Again and again, Nietzsche shifts the discussion away from strength to perception, as he had with the cripples and beggars at the great bridge. It is not a particular victor, or identity, or outcome that interests Nietzsche, but the willingness to move away from the triumph of the winners, from someone else's description of your self, and away from the comforts of home. This spur to new knowledge is what characterizes the free spirits. This philosophy is best understood through Nietzsche's literary creation, Zarathustra, the free spirit who strives to be superman.

Nietzsche based the figure of Zarathustra, the figure through which he would speak his philosophy, on Zoroaster, the Persian prophet of the sixth century BCE. According to Nietzsche, Zoroaster had been the first to see the world in terms of good and evil. But if Zoroaster created "this most calamitous error," it would be Nietzsche's Zarathustra who would undo it. Zarathustra's mission was thus: "the self-overcoming of morality, out of truthfulness; the self-overcoming of the moralist, into his opposite—into me—that is what the name Zarathustra means in my mouth."[37] Zarathustra is the wanderer who speaks, who strains in his journeys to move beyond good and evil and to expose morality to the townspeople in the market square. Why does he seek out others and speak so insistently? Why does he care to tell his message to the herd? In the end, Nietzsche believes that the herd might be transformed. It is precisely human beings who have been the creators and free spirits throughout history. They have distinguished themselves from animals, named their world, invented myths to live by, and even imposed on themselves conceptions of morality, including that of good and evil. For all the weight they carry, for their "human, all too human" limitations, it is human beings, and no other form of life, who have shown themselves to be "gay" and audacious. Nietzsche regards the human as "the rare exception," the animal who has "not yet been determined" (see Document 7, section 62). "Truth is there: after all, the people are there!" Zarathustra concludes with cosmic optimism.[38]

There are three figures in Nietzsche's writings who characterize the superman and help us understand who he is: the annihilator, the dancer, and the child. It is the annihilator who breaks old tablets. Nietzsche wants his readers to see the pieces of morality's broken tablets on the ground (see Document 6, "On Old and New Tablets"). All the old rules are to be annulled. Do not "act 'for your neighbor'" Zarathustra urges. "Plug up your ears" when you hear moral authority demand that you do things "'for' and 'in order' and 'because.'" Living virtuously means that the individual should not bend her will and his desire to the expectations of neighbors, but to love the self: "You are pregnant only with your own child."[39]

There is something belligerent about this uncompromising annihilator. Zarathustra is in many ways a Moses-like figure, smashing tablets rather than revealing them, as Moses had, or clinging to the mountainside to climb higher and higher to new heights. Nietzsche colludes in this impression, acknowledging the "non-adorer who dwells in the woods" to be "as hateful to the people as a wolf to dogs."[40] Indeed, "it is the good war that hallows any cause," Nietzsche writes in one of the lines that thousands of young men read and memorized in the trenches of World War I, when German military officials distributed mass-produced editions of *Thus Spoke Zarathustra* to the frontlines. But Nietzsche is not talking about a German war against France, or a military action for any cause. In fact, Zarathustra condemns all moralities that mobilize individuals to serve a greater good whether that good is on behalf of neighbors, the public, or the nation. The "short peace" that Nietzsche prefers is simply a provisional or transitional place from which free spirits move on, struggling with the satisfactions and certainties of the moment and trying to topple the idols that peace and stability maintain.[41] To be at war is to be restless, to be at peace is to stand still. In this sense, the warrior is simply the truth-seeker, whereas the former warriors who have sheathed their knives believe they possess the truth and are no longer interested in or fit for the difficult journey to a thousand "hidden isles of life." In Nietzsche's view, they have blinked.

The restlessness Nietzsche honors is also introduced by another figure who appears repeatedly in *Zarathustra*, and it displaces the image of the angry prophet. This is the figure of the dancer who takes many steps, joyously, playfully, without really going anywhere in particular. "Yes, I recognize Zarathustra. [. . .] Doesn't he walk like a dancer?" (see Document 6, "Prologue," section 2), which is to say he moves without purpose, or "crookedly," and thereby evades the nets of custom and common sense. The dancer's opposite is the statue, "stiff, stupid, and stony," a "column" in the temple of moral authority.[42] What dancing represents for Nietzsche is a glimpse of the "impossible as possible," the defiance of the "spirit of gravity," the effort to escape the frozen identities of statues, which belong to canonizers and deifiers.[43] The dancer is a wonderful means to capture the unceasing, constantly turning quest for new knowledge and new ways of looking at things. He is a good figure to have on the way to becoming superman because he is unwilling to blink or stand still and is ready to set off on and endure the restless journey of recreating the self.

In addition to the annihilator, who is the breaker of tablets, and the dancer, who dances playfully between the stiff statues of history, there is a third figure whom Zarathustra introduces as his own, the child. The famous parable of "the three metamorphoses," in which the free "spirit becomes a camel, the camel a lion, and the lion, finally, a child," indicates the importance of obtaining a new innocence. If there is a destination for Nietzsche, it is the place from which to see the world once more in the eyes of the child. The naiveté of the child proposes what J. P. Stern calls a "sophisticated breakthrough into unsophistication," in which myths are happily believed and new cultural activity takes place.[44] Although much of Zarathustra's energy is spent climbing over life, the child leaves room for the acquisition of new myths and new gods.

In Zarathustra's speech "on the three metamorphoses of the spirit," the first two are pretty clear (see Document 6). First is the camel, an animal well-adapted to take up the burdens of truth-seeking in the desert, which is far removed from the satisfactions of society, and second is the lion, whose strong spirit can oppose "thou shalt" with "I will" and do battle with the "last god," the god of monotheism. But "to create new values—not even the lion can do that." This task of creation is left to the child, for "the child is innocence, and forgetting, a new beginning" (see Document 6, "On the Three Metamorphoses"). Unlike the camel and the lion, the child does not leave behind or fight what is old, but wakes up to a completely new reality without the memory of having abandoned an older version, which the camel and lion still retain. With the metamorphosis into the child, the free spirit exists inside a new myth without the self-defeating knowledge that the universe is just something made up and thus still possesses the complete confidence of living vigorously. "The man who has been lost in the world now conquers *his own* world" (see Document 6, "On the Three Metamorphoses"). This is Nietzsche's "philosophy of the morning."[45]

Many modern-day commentators are not impressed with the final metamorphosis of the free spirit into the innocent child. They charge Nietzsche with inconsistency and prefer his image of the dancer. The objection is that the child does not and cannot have the difficult historical knowledge of the origins of morality and of the fundamentally fictional nature of describing and redescribing the universe and is thus not a satisfying embodiment of superman. According to the American philosopher Richard Rorty, with the spirit's final metamorphosis, Nietzsche has "fobbed us off with the suggestion" that the child will "have all the advantages of thought with none of the disadvantages of speaking some particular language."[46] Rorty concludes that reading Nietzsche is good for individuals to think through in order "to make the best selves for ourselves we can" through the continual activity of redescription, basically the business of the camel and the lion.[47] But Nietzsche's writings are not a useful guide to creating a good and just society, and Rorty has little patience with the invitation to construct new myths via the child's innocence because they undo all the excavating work that Nietzsche has made such an effort to undertake in order to expose myths. However, Nietzsche himself is in fact very much taken with the idea of creating new myths for society to live by and even inventing new gods to inhabit those myths. Although Zarathustra refers to "overmen" or "supermen" wandering in ones and twos, Nietzsche also hints that the trickle of free spirits in the present might turn into a rushing stream in the future. He refers to "premature births of an as yet unproven future" and to the "first-born of the twentieth century."[48] These images suggest that Nietzsche is thinking of a new, insistently collective shape to the future. All the talk about children and the new dawn they represent points to Nietz-sche's hope that a new myth-filled existence will replace contempo-rary civilization, that the dice will be rolled again, and that the world will look completely different as a result.

However, when Nietzsche had a chance to embrace a new myth for nineteenth-century Germany, he repudiated it. In the early 1870s, when Nietzsche began his philosophical work and celebrated the vibrant culture of ancient Greece, he formed a close friendship with the German composer Richard Wagner, whom he took to be a cultural prophet who might break with the Christian morality of his day. For a time, Nietzsche believed that Wagner and his grand ring or cycle of operas that featured medieval Germanic heroes provided a glimpse of new, modern myths to live by. In texts such as "On the Uses and Dis-advantages of History for Life" (1874) he repeatedly called for new exemplars and new spurs to greatness. But if Nietzsche initially believed that Wagner's art represented "the path of a German pagan-ism . . . a specifically un-Christian way of viewing the world," Nietz-sche's actual exposure to Wagner's artistic circle at Bayreuth in newly unified Germany in 1876 convinced him that Wagner and his support-ers were simply enthralled with a hyperventilated, self-satisfied Ger-man nationalism.[49] Full of regrets, Nietzsche cut his ties to Wagner and redirected his energies to uncovering the origins of moral codes and underscoring the erroneous, tendentious, and even conformist aspect to all collective interpretations of reality. Nietzsche never aban-doned the figure of the child, or the prospect of new myths and new gods, but almost everything Nietzsche wrote in the 1880s up to the moment of his final madness was directed against the development of a particular identity and against the experience of a single authentic, statuesque self. Nietzsche lauds the act of creation, but does so as the premise for further movement; he values differentiation, but in order to admit the foreign and strange.

NIETZSCHE'S LEGACY

Nietzsche's general celebration of the world-making ability of cultures, his criticism of the spiritual emptiness of the contemporary world, and his initial exaltation of Wagner as a source of modern myth preoccu-pied the reception of Nietzsche's work in the two decades after World War I. It was not the unblinking individual, but the unfulfilled collec-tive that was the object of general attention. Moreover, in Germany,

Nietzsche's contempt for the idea of global humanity reinforced the tendency to see German history as a special path from the catastrophe of military defeat to the redemption of total victory. Enthralled readers in Germany itself and curious half-alarmed readers elsewhere in Europe consistently interpreted Nietzsche's myths as national myths designed to propel Germany to greatness. Thousands of German soldiers fought in World War I with *Thus Spoke Zarathustra* in their knapsacks. Not surprisingly, after World War I, the Nazis appropriated Nietzsche and elevated *Thus Spoke Zarathustra* into a canonical Aryan text. Along with Adolf Hitler's *Mein Kampf* and Alfred Rosenberg's *Myth of the Twentieth Century*, it was placed in the vault of the memorial to Germany's victory over the Russians in 1914 at Tannenberg, in East Prussia.[50] For the Nazis, who attempted to accomplish nothing less than the generation of a new Aryan man to live heroically and vigorously in a German empire that would enslave or eliminate vanquished peoples and who wanted to replace the mercy of Christian morality with the pitilessness of Aryan morality, there was much to draw from in Nietzsche's writings, and they were encouraged in this by Nietzsche's sister, Elizabeth Förster-Nietzsche, until her death in 1935.

Given Nietzsche's outspoken attack on anti-Semitism and on essential or authentic identities, Nietzsche is misplaced as a Nazi prophet. Yet his insistence on the value of creating new rules to live by, his enthusiasm for new kinds of strong men, his acceptance of violent political campaigns in the case of the ancient Greeks, and his general contempt for those who cast their lives in terms of suffering suggest how easy it was for readers in the interwar period to nazify Nietzsche. Moreover, doesn't Nietzsche's call for society to invent new myths, whatever their content, authorize the Nazi experiment, whatever its content? Steven Aschheim provides an initial answer when he points out that "Nietzsche's determinedly shifting narrative point of view clearly facilitated varied appropriations."[51] If Nietzsche is read one way, the philosopher commends the critical, restless spirit of the dancer, a very non-Nazi image. Yet Nietzsche refers repeatedly even in his later texts to the value of new beginnings and mythic enclosures, which comes much closer to including the radical differentiation the Nazis aspired to. Thus, the flip side of the angry announcement "God is dead" is the creative, amoral exhortation "decide for yourselves," "invent your gods." All this justifies some link between Nietzsche and the Nazis.

However, the main thrust of Nietzsche's thought is not the urge to kill gods or to invent them. His emphasis is on perspective, which is why he makes so much of the state of wakefulness, condemns the weak willed who blink, and cherishes how men and women have created for themselves their own new eyes "and ever again new eyes." It is this Nietzsche, who poses responsibilities for the self, who inspired existentialist thinkers in France in the 1930s and 1940s. It was in this light that the American philosopher Walter Kaufmann provided authoritative English translations of Nietzsche beginning in the 1950s, as well as extensive commentaries that still circulate in college classrooms today. Nietzsche's perspectivism also heavily influenced contemporary philosophers such as Michel Foucault, Jacques Derrida, and Richard Rorty.

Nietzsche's attention to both the contingency of knowledge and the possibility of new angles of perception remains a highly pertinent topic in the debates about truth, ethics, and representation. Nietzsche remains so radical because he does not operate inside the dominant rational and scientific framework of the modern era, which holds that critical thought and scientific method are actually revealing the state of the world. Rather, he ascertains that all cultures and all peoples live inside the languages and perspectives and myths they have fashioned, and that these forms are both life enhancing and life denying and are both authoritative and breakable. Moreover, the search for "the" truth is misguided, and the expectation for complete clarity is impossible. Truth is not obtainable because meaning has to be produced by human beings in their own vocabularies, and these meanings will be utterly different. That superman at one point speaks in a stammer poignantly indicates the sheer effort of the individual to say something new about the world: "Then speak and stammer, 'This is *my* good; this I love [. . .] I do not want it as divine law; I do not want it as human statue.'"[52] The stammerer is a fitting image with which to conclude this introduction. It recalls Nietzsche's overriding interest not in defining the world in any particular way but in telling his readers that the world we know is encompassed by ordinary language; that it is a hard struggle to think in new ways because we speak in "old tongues"; and that any such struggle is intense and highly personal and difficult to translate. The stammerer displaces superman and his strength, and restores to view the overman who struggles with new sounds and new possibilities. New knowledge is only expressed in a stammer, and Nietzsche insists on complete wakefulness to hear it.

NOTES

[1] Joseph Viktor Widmann, "Nietzsche's Dangerous Book," Tim Hyde and Lysane Fauvel, trans. *New Nietzsche Studies* 4 (2000), pp. 195–200, here p. 195.

[2] Friedrich Nietzsche, *On the Genealogy of Morals* and *Ecce Homo*, Walter Kaufmann, trans. and ed. (New York: Random House, 1967), p. 226.

[3] Stefan Zweig, *Master Builders: A Typology of the Spirit* (New York: Viking, 1939), p. 445.

[4] Friedrich Nietzsche, "Das Kind mit dem Spiegel," *Also Sprach Zarathustra*, Kritische Studienausgabe, Giorgio Colli and Mazzino Montinari, eds. (Berlin: De Gruyter, 1967ff), vol. 4, p. 107; also translated as "The Child with the Mirror," *Thus Spoke Zarathustra*, Walter Kaufmann, trans. (New York: Viking, 1966), p. 84.

[5] J. P. Stern, *Friedrich Nietzsche* (New York: Penguin, 1979), pp. 95–96.

[6] Friedrich Nietzsche, *Götzen-Dämmerung, oder Wie man mit dem Hammer philosophirt*, Kritische Studienausgabe, Giorgio Colli and Mazzino Montinari, eds. (Berlin: De Gruyter, 1967ff), vol. 6, p. 55; also translated as "Twilight of the Idols, or How One Philosophizes with a Hammer," in Walter Kaufmann, ed. and trans., *The Portable Nietzsche* (New York: Viking, 1954), p. 463.

[7] R. J. Hollingdale, *Nietzsche: The Man and His Philosophy*, rev. ed. (Cambridge: Cambridge University Press, 1999), p. 118.

[8] David B. Allison, *Reading the New Nietzsche* (New York: Rowman & Littlefield, 2001), p. 76.

[9] Section 125, Friedrich Nietzsche, *Die fröhliche Wissenschaft*, Kritische Studienausgabe, Giorgio Colli and Mazzino Montinari, eds. (Berlin: De Gruyter, 1967ff), vol. 3, pp. 480–81, also translated as *The Gay Science*, trans. Walter Kaufmann (New York: Vintage, 1974), p. 182.

[10] Section 335, Friedrich Nietzsche, *Die fröhliche Wissenschaft*, Kritische Studienausgabe, Giorgio Colli and Mazzino Montinari, eds. (Berlin: De Gruyter, 1967ff), vol. 3, p. 562; also translated as *The Gay Science*, trans. Walter Kaufmann (New York: Vintage, 1974), p. 264.

[11] Section 33, Friedrich Nietzsche, *Die fröhliche Wissenschaft*, Kritische Studienausgabe, Giorgio Colli and Mazzino Montinari, eds. (Berlin: De Gruyter, 1967ff), vol. 3, p. 404; also translated as *The Gay Science*, p. 104.

[12] Nietzsche, "Vom Land der Bildung," *Also Sprach Zarathustra*, vol. 4, p. 155; also translated as "On the Land of Education," *Thus Spoke Zarathustra*, p. 121.

[13] Friedrich Nietzsche, Section 44, "Sprüche und Pfeile," *Götzen-Dämmerung*, Kritische Studienausgabe, Giorgio Colli and Mazzino Montinari, eds. (Berlin: De Gruyter, 1967ff), vol. 6, also translated as "Twilight of the Idols," trans. R. J. Hollingdale (Cambridge: Cambridge University Press, 1997).

[14] Section 343, Friedrich Nietzsche, *Die fröhliche Wissenschaft*, Kritische Studienausgabe, Giorgio Colli and Mazzino Montinari, eds. (Berlin: De Gruyter, 1967ff), vol. 3, p. 574, also translated as *The Gay Science*, trans. Walter Kaufmann (New York: Vintage, 1974), p. 280.

[15] Nietzsche, "Von der schenkenden Tugend," *Also Sprach Zarathustra*, vol. 4, p. 102; also translated as "On the Gift-giving Virtue," *Thus Spoke Zarathustra*, p. 78.

[16] Nietzsche, "Von der schenkenden Tugend," *Also Sprach Zarathustra*, vol. 4, p. 100; also translated as "On the Gift-giving Virtue," *Thus Spoke Zarathustra*, p. 77.

[17] Nietzsche, "Vom neuen Götzen," *Also Sprach Zarathustra*, vol. 4, p. 61; also translated as "On the New Idol," *Thus Spoke Zarathustra*, p. 49.

[18] Nietzsche, *Götzen-Dämmerung*, vol. 6, p. 96; also translated as "Twilight of the Idols," *Portable Nietzsche*, p. 500.

[19] Nietzsche, "Von der Nächstenliebe," *Also Sprach Zarathustra*, vol. 4, p. 77; also translated as "On Love of the Neighbor," *Thus Spoke Zarathustra*, p. 60.

[20] Section 14, Friedrich Nietzsche, *Jenseits von Gut und Böse*, Kritische Studienausgabe, Giorgio Colli and Mazzino Montinari, eds. (Berlin: De Gruyter, 1967ff), vol. 5,

p. 28; also translated as *Beyond Good and Evil*, Walter Kaufmann, trans. (New York: Random House, 1966), p. 33.

[21]Section 16, Friedrich Nietzsche, *Morgenröthe*, Kritische Studienausgabe, Giorgio Colli and Mazzino Montinari, eds. (Berlin: De Gruyter, 1967ff), vol. 3, p. 29; also translated as *Daybreak*, R. J. Hollingdale, trans. (Cambridge: Cambridge University Press, 1997), p. 15.

[22]See section 24, Friedrich Nietzsche, *Jenseits von Gut und Böse*, Kritische Studienausgabe, Giorgio Colli and Mazzino Montinari, eds. (Berlin: De Gruyter, 1967ff), vol. 5, p. 42; also translated as *Beyond Good and Evil*, Walter Kaufmann, trans. (New York: Random House, 1966), p. 35.

[23]Section 24, Friedrich Nietzsche, *Jenseits von Gut und Böse*, Kritische Studienausgabe, Giorgio Colli and Mazzino Montinari, eds. (Berlin: De Gruyter, 1967ff), vol. 5, p. 41; also translated as *Beyond Good and Evil*, Walter Kaufmann, trans. (New York: Random House, 1966), p. 35.

[24]Nietzsche, "Von der berühmten Weisen," *Also Sprach Zarathustra*, vol. 4, p. 132; also translated as "On the Famous Wise Men," *Thus Spoke Zarathustra*, p. 102.

[25]Section 2, Friedrich Nietzsche, *Der Antichrist*, Kritische Studienausgabe, Giorgio Colli and Mazzino Montinari, eds. (Berlin: De Gruyter, 1967ff), vol. 6, p. 170; also translated as "The Antichrist," *Portable Nietzsche*, p. 570.

[26]See also section 24, Nietzsche, "Von alten und neuen Tafeln," *Also Sprach Zarathustra*, vol. 4, p. 264, also translated as "On Old and New Tablets," *Thus Spoke Zarathustra*, p. 211.

[27]Section 25, Friedrich Nietzsche, *Der Antichrist*, Kritische Studienausgabe, Giorgio Colli and Mazzino Montinari, eds. (Berlin: De Gruyter, 1967ff), vol. 6, p. 194; also translated as "The Antichrist," *Portable Nietzsche*, p. 595.

[28]Section 14, third essay, *Zur Genealogie der Moral*, Kritische Studienausgabe, Giorgio Colli and Mazzino Montinari, eds. (Berlin: De Gruyter, 1967ff), vol. 5, p. 367; also translated as *On the Genealogy of Morals*, Walter Kaufmann, trans. (New York: Random House, 1967), p. 121.

[29]Section 46, Friedrich Nietzsche, *Jenseits von Gut und Böse*, Kritische Studienausgabe, Giorgio Colli and Mazzino Montinari, eds. (Berlin, 1967ff), vol. 5, p. 66; also translated as *Beyond Good and Evil*, Walter Kaufmann, trans. (New York: Random House, 1966), p. 60.

[30]Section 18, third essay, *Zur Genealogie der Moral*, Kritische Studienausgabe, Giorgio Colli and Mazzino Montinari, eds. (Berlin: De Gruyter, 1967ff), vol. 5, p. 383; also translated as *On the Genealogy of Morals*, Walter Kaufmann, trans. (New York: Random House, 1967), p. 135.

[31]Section 46, Friedrich Nietzsche, *Jenseits von Gut und Böse*, Kritische Studienausgabe, Giorgio Colli and Mazzino Montinari, eds. (Berlin: De Gruyter, 1967ff), vol. 5, p. 67; also translated as *Beyond Good and Evil*, Walter Kaufmann, trans. (New York: Random House, 1966), p. 60.

[32]Section 46, Friedrich Nietzsche, *Jenseits von Gut und Böse*, Kritische Studienausgabe, Giorgio Colli and Mazzino Montinari, eds. (Berlin: De Gruyter, 1967ff), vol. 5, p. 67; also translated as *Beyond Good and Evil*, Walter Kaufmann, trans. (New York: Random House, 1966), p. 61.

[33]Section 199, Friedrich Nietzsche, *Jenseits von Gut und Böse*, Kritische Studienausgabe, Giorgio Colli and Mazzino Montinari, eds. (Berlin, 1967ff), vol. 5, p. 120; also translated as *Beyond Good and Evil*, Walter Kaufmann, trans. (New York, 1966), p. 111.

[34]Nietzsche, "Vom neuen Götzen," *Also Sprach Zarathustra*, vol. 4, p. 61; also translated as "On the New Idol," *Thus Spoke Zarathustra*, p. 49.

[35]Section 60, Nietzsche, *Der Antichrist*, Kritische Studienausgabe, Giorgio Colli and Mazzino Montinari, eds. (Berlin: De Gruyter, 1967ff), vol. 6, p. 249; also translated as "The Antichrist," *Portable Nietzsche*, p. 652.

[36]Friedrich Nietzsche, "Vom Nutzen und Nachtheil der Historie für das Leben," *Unzeitgemässe Betrachtungen*, Kritische Studienausgabe, Giorgio Colli and Mazzino

Montinari, eds. (Berlin: De Gruyter, 1967ff), vol. 1, pp. 274, 282; also translated as "On the Uses and Disadvantages of History for Life," *Untimely Meditations*, R. J. Hollingdale, trans. (Cambridge: Cambridge University Press, 1997), pp. 79, 85.

[37]Section 3, Friedrich Nietzsche, *Ecce Homo*, Kritische Studienausgabe, Giorgio Colli and Mazzino Montinari, eds. (Berlin: De Gruyter, 1967ff), vol. 6, p. 367; also translated as "Why I Am a Destiny," *Ecce Homo*, Walter Kaufmann, trans. (New York: Vintage, 1967), pp. 327–28.

[38]Nietzsche, "Von den berühmten Weisen," *Also Sprach Zarathustra*, vol. 4, p. 132; also translated as "On the Famous Wise Man," *Thus Spoke Zarathustra*, p. 103.

[39]Section 11, Nietzsche, "Vom höheren Menschen," *Also Sprach Zarathustra*, vol. 4, p. 362; also translated as "On the Higher Man," *Thus Spoke Zarathustra*, pp. 290–91.

[40]Nietzsche, "Von der berühmten Weisen," *Also Sprach Zarathustra*, vol. 4, p. 132; also translated as "On the Famous Wise Men," *Thus Spoke Zarathustra*, p. 102.

[41]Nietzsche, "Vom Krieg und Kriegsvolk," *Also Sprach Zarathustra*, vol. 4, pp. 58–59; also translated as "On War and Warriors," *Thus Spoke Zarathustra*, p. 47.

[42]Section 17, Nietzsche, "Vom höheren Menschen," *Also Sprach Zarathustra*, vol. 4, p. 366; also translated as "On the Famous Wise Man," *Thus Spoke Zarathustra*, p. 294.

[43]Section 1: 206, Friedrich Nietzsche, *Menschliches, Allzumenschliches*, Kritische Studienausgabe, Giorgio Colli and Mazzino Montinari, eds. (Berlin: De Gruyter, 1967ff), vol. 2, p. 170; also translated as *Human, All Too Human*, R. J. Hollingdale, trans. (Cambridge: Cambridge University Press, 1986), p. 96; and Nietzsche, "Vom Lesen und Schreiben," *Also Sprach Zarathustra*, vol. 4, p. 49; also translated as "On Reading and Writing," *Thus Spoke Zarathustra*, p. 41.

[44]J. P. Stern, *Friedrich Nietzsche* (New York: Penguin, 1979), p. 50.

[45]Section 1: 638, Friedrich Nietzsche, *Menschliches, Allzumenschliches*, Kritische Studienausgabe, Giorgio Colli and Mazzino Montinari, eds. (Berlin: De Gruyter, 1967ff), vol. 2, p. 363; also translated as *Human, All Too Human*, R. J. Hollingdale, trans. (Cambridge: Cambridge University Press, 1986), p. 204.

[46]Richard Rorty, *Contingency, Irony, and Solidarity* (Cambridge: Cambridge University Press, 1989), p. 112.

[47]Richard Rorty, *Contingency, Irony, and Solidarity* (Cambridge: Cambridge University Press, 1989), p. 80.

[48]Section 382, Nietzsche, *Die fröhliche Wissenschaft*, Kritische Studienausgabe, Giorgio Colli and Mazzino Montinari, eds. (Berlin: De Gruyter, 1967ff), vol. 3, p. 635; also translated as *The Gay Science*, Walter Kaufmann, trans. (New York: Vintage, 1974), p. 346; and Section 214, Friedrich Nietzsche, *Jenseits von Gut und Böse*, Kritische Studienausgabe, Giorgio Colli and Mazzino Montinari, eds. (Berlin: De Gruyter, 1967ff), vol. 5, p. 151; also translated as *Beyond Good and Evil*, Walter Kaufmann, trans. (New York: Random House, 1966), p. 145.

[49]George S. Williamson, *The Longing for Myth in Germany: Religion and Aesthetic Culture from Romanticism to Nietzsche* (Chicago: University of Chicago Press, 2004), p. 274.

[50]Steven E. Aschheim, *The Nietzsche Legacy in Germany, 1890–1990* (Berkeley: University of California Press, 1992), p. 239.

[51]Steven E. Aschheim, *The Nietzsche Legacy in Germany, 1890–1990* (Berkeley: University of California Press, 1992), p. 8.

[52]Nietzsche, "Von den Freuden- und Leidenschaften," *Also Sprach Zarathustra*, vol. 4, p. 42; also translated as "On Enjoying and Suffering the Passions," *Thus Spoke Zarathustra*, p. 36.

PART TWO

The Documents

1

Aphorisms

1875–1889

Nietzsche loved paradoxes and believed that they offered much better points of entry into the ways of the world than did rational explanations—just consider the title of one collection from which many of the aphorisms below are drawn: Human, All Too Human *(1878). The last three words qualify or twist the meaning evoked by the first. Aphorisms are pithy statements or opinions along the lines of Nietzsche's most famous saying that "what does not destroy me, makes me stronger,"[1] but most of Nietzsche's aphorisms reveal hidden meanings; for example, they lead the reader from "human" to "all too human." Nietzsche's aphoristic style works well in the service of his philosophy, which is intended to shatter the conventional meaning of words and to suggest alternative interpretations. His aphorisms develop and elaborate the possibilities of life. They are scattered throughout his writings and readers will encounter more in the selections from* Thus Spoke Zarathustra *included in this volume. Since Nietzsche's aphorisms often rest on contradictions, they require a careful reading or deciphering, which their brevity does not always invite. They do not state the truth, but play with it; they are dangerous little flirtations.*

Enemies of truth. Convictions are more dangerous enemies of truth than lies.[2]

Ultimate skepticism. In the end, what are the truths of mankind? They are the *irrefutable* errors of mankind.[3]

---

[1]Section 8, "Sprüche und Pfeile," *Götzen-Dämmerung*, Kritische Studienausgabe, Giorgio Colli and Mazzino Montinari, eds. (Berlin: De Gruyter, 1967ff), vol. 6, p. 60.
[2]Volume 1: 483, Section 483, "Des Mensch mit sich allein," Friedrich Nietzsche, *Menschliches, Allzumenschliches*, Kritische Studienausgabe, Giorgio Colli and Mazzino Montinari, eds. (Berlin: De Gruyter, 1967ff), vol. 2, p. 317.
[3]Section 265, Friedrich Nietzsche, *Die fröhliche Wissenschaft*, Kritischc Studienausgabe, Giorgio Colli and Mazzino Montinari, eds. (Berlin: De Gruyter, 1967ff), vol. 3, p. 518.

There are no moral phenomena, only a moral interpretation of phenomena.[4]

Opinions form out of *passions*; *sheer laziness* lets these harden into *convictions*.[5]

How language endangers spiritual freedom. —Every word is a prejudice.[6]

I am afraid we will not get rid of God because we still believe in grammar . . .[7]

Lack of Friends. To lack of friends suggests envy or arrogance. Many a man owes his friends simply to the fortunate circumstances that he gives them no cause for envy.[8]

To those who are praised. As long as you are being praised, you need to remember that you are not yet on your own path, but on someone else's.[9]

Bad Memory. The advantage of bad memory is that you can enjoy the same good things for the first time many times over.[10]

Fifteen Minutes Earlier. Occasionally we encounter someone whose views are ahead of his time, but only to the extent that he anticipates

[4]Section 108, Friedrich Nietzsche, *Jenseits von Gut und Böse*, Kritische Studienausgabe, Giorgio Colli and Mazzino Montinari, eds. (Berlin: De Gruyter, 1967ff), vol. 5, p. 92.

[5]Section 637, "Des Mensch mit sich allein," Friedrich Nietzsche, *Menschliches, Allzumenschliches*, Kritische Studienausgabe, Giorgio Colli and Mazzino Montinari, eds. (Berlin: De Gruyter, 1967ff), vol. 2, p. 362. This is the opening line of a longer paragraph.

[6]Section 55, "Der Wanderer und sein Schatten," Friedrich Nietzsche, *Menschliches, Allzumenschliches*, Kritische Studienausgabe, Giorgio Colli and Mazzino Montinari, eds. (Berlin: De Gruyter, 1967ff), vol. 2, p. 577.

[7]Section 5, "Die 'Vernunft' in der Philosophie," Friedrich Nietzsche, *Götzen-Dämmerung*, Kritische Studienausgabe, Giorgio Colli and Mazzino Montinari, eds. (Berlin: De Gruyter, 1967ff), vol. 6, p. 78. This is the closing line of a longer paragraph.

[8]Section 559, "Der Mensch mit sich allein," Friedrich Nietzsche, *Menschliches, Allzumenschliches*, Kritische Studienausgabe, Giorgio Colli and Mazzino Montinari, eds. (Berlin: De Gruyter, 1967ff), vol. 2, p. 331.

[9]Section 340, "Vermischte Meinungen und Sprüche," Friedrich Nietzsche, *Menschliches, Allzumenschliches*, Kritische Studienausgabe, Giorgio Colli and Mazzino Montinari, eds. (Berlin: De Gruyter, 1967ff), vol. 2, p. 518.

[10]Section 580, "Der Mensch mit sich allein," Friedrich Nietzsche, *Menschliches, Allzumenschliches*, Kritische Studienausgabe, Giorgio Colli and Mazzino Montinari, eds. (Berlin: De Gruyter, 1967ff), vol. 2, p. 580.

the tasteless views of the next ten years. He anticipates public opinion before it is public, that is to say, he has succumbed to what will surely be a trivial view fifteen minutes before the others have. His fame usually tends to be much noisier than the fame of the truly great and superior.[11]

Against Originals. When art dresses itself in the most worn-out material, it is most easily recognized as art.[12]

War. Against war it can be said: it makes the victors stupid and the vanquished spiteful. For war it can be said: with these two effects, it barbarizes man and thereby makes him more natural. In war, a culture hibernates and winters and mankind emerges stronger, for good and evil.[13]

The wise man as astronomer. — As long as you still think of the stars as something "above you," you will lack the eye of knowledge.[14]

Doors. The child, like the man, sees doors in everything he experiences and learns, but for the one they are *entrances*, for the other only *throughways*.[15]

A man's maturity — that means to have found once again the seriousness one had as a child, at play.[16]

[11]Section 269, "Anzeichen höherer und niederer kultur," Friedrich Nietzsche, *Menschliches, Allzumenschliches*, Kritische Studienausgabe, Giorgio Colli and Mazzino Montinari, eds. (Berlin: De Gruyter, 1967ff), vol. 2, pp. 222–23.

[12]Section 179, "Aus der Seele der Künstler und Schriftsteller," Friedrich Nietzsche, *Menschliches, Allzumenschliches*, Kritische Studienausgabe, Giorgio Colli and Mazzino Montinari, eds. (Berlin: De Gruyter, 1967ff), vol. 2, p. 162.

[13]Section 444, "Ein Blick auf den Stoat," Friedrich Nietzsche, *Menschliches, Allzumenschliches*, Kritische Studienausgabe, Giorgio Colli and Mazzino Montinari, eds. (Berlin: De Gruyter, 1967ff), vol. 2, p. 289.

[14]Section 71, Friedrich Nietzsche, *Jenseits von Gut und Böse*, Kritische Studienausgabe, Giorgio Colli and Mazzino Montinari, eds. (Berlin: De Gruyter, 1967ff), vol. 5, p. 86.

[15]Section 281, "Vermischte Meinungen und Sprüche," Friedrich Nietzsche, *Menschliches, Allzumenschliches*, Kritische Studienausgabe, Giorgio Colli and Mazzino Montinari, eds. (Berlin: De Gruyter, 1967ff), vol. 2, p. 496.

[16]Section 94, Friedrich Nietzsche, *Jenseits von Gut und Böse*, Kritische Studienausgabe, Giorgio Colli and Mazzino Montinari, eds. (Berlin: De Gruyter, 1967ff), vol. 5, p. 90.

Feelings and Their Origin in Judgment. "Trust your feelings!"—But feelings are not final or original; behind feelings there are the judgments and value statements you have inherited in the form of feelings (inclinations, aversions). The inspiration that originates out of feeling is the grandson of a judgment, often a false judgment, and in any case not your own child! To trust your feelings—that means to obey your grandfather and your grandmother and their grandparents more than you would *your own* gods, your reason and your experience.[17]

God's Conditions. "God himself cannot exist without wise people," said Luther[18] with good reason; but "God certainly cannot exist without unwise people"—that our good Luther did not say![19]

A dangerous determination. The Christian determination to find that the world is ugly and bad has made the world ugly and bad.[20]

The problem I pose here is not what should succeed mankind in the sequence of living things (man is an *end*), but rather what sort of man we should *cultivate*, we should *will* as being more valuable, more worthy of life, more certain of the future. This more valuable type has existed often enough already, but as a lucky accident, as an exception, never as something *willed*. In fact, *he* has been the creature most dreaded, almost *the dreadful* itself, and out of dread the opposite was willed, cultivated, and *achieved*: the household pet, the herd animal, the sick animal man—the Christian.[21]

Origins of Faith. The fettered spirit does not take up his position out of conviction, but from habit. For example, he is a Christian, not because he had knowledge of the various religions and chose among them; he is an Englishman, not because he decided in favor of England. Rather, he came across Christianity and Englishness and accepted them with-

---

[17]Section 35, Friedrich Nietzsche, *Morgenröthe*, Kritische Studienausgabe, Giorgio Colli and Mazzino Montinari, eds. (Berlin: De Gruyter, 1967ff), vol. 3, pp. 43–44.

[18]*Luther:* Martin Luther (1483–1546), the German monk and theologian whose break with the authority of the papacy in Rome ushered in the Reformation and the development of Protestantism.

[19]Section 129, Friedrich Nietzsche, *Die fröhliche Wissenschaft*, Kritische Studienausgabe, Giorgio Colli and Mazzino Montinari, eds. (Berlin: De Gruyter, 1967ff), vol. 3, pp. 484–85.

[20]Section 130, Friedrich Nietzsche, *Die fröhliche Wissenschaft*, Kritische Studienausgabe, Giorgio Colli and Mazzino Montinari, eds. (Berlin: De Gruyter, 1967ff), vol. 3, p. 485.

[21]Section 3, Friedrich Nietzsche, *Der Antichrist*, Kritische Studienausgabe, Giorgio Colli and Mazzino Montinari, eds. (Berlin: De Gruyter, 1967ff), vol. 6, p. 170.

out any reasons, just like someone born in wine country who becomes a wine drinker. Later on, perhaps, when he was a Christian or an Englishman, he found a few reasons to defend his habit, but if these reasons are refuted, his general position is not. For example, when a fettered spirit is asked to state his reasons for objecting to bigamy, it becomes clear whether his holy zeal for monogamy rests on reason or habit. The adoption of spiritual principles without reason is called faith.[22]

My task! It is to make individuals *uncomfortable*.[23]

What will seal the freedom we have attained?—no longer to be ashamed in front of ourselves.[24]

Formula for my happiness: a Yes, a No, a straight line, a *goal*.[25]

[22]Section 226, "Anzeichen höherer und niederer kultur," Friedrich Nietzsche, *Menschliches, Allzumenschliches*, Kritische Studienausgabe, Giorgio Colli and Mazzino Montinari, eds. (Berlin: De Gruyter, 1967ff), vol. 2, p. 190.
[23]Friedrich Nietzsche, "Nachgelassene Fragmente," spring/summer 1875, 5 [178], Kritische Studienausgabe, Giorgio Colli and Mazzino Montinari, eds. (Berlin: De Gruyter, 1967ff), vol. 8, p. 91.
[24]Section 275, Friedrich Nietzsche, *Die fröhliche Wissenschaft*, Kritische Studienausgabe, Giorgio Colli and Mazzino Montinari, eds. (Berlin: De Gruyter, 1967ff), vol. 3, p. 519.
[25]Section 44, "Sprüche und Pfeile," Friedrich Nietzsche, *Götzen-Dämmerung*, Kritische Studienausgabe, Giorgio Colli and Mazzino Montinari, eds. (Berlin: De Gruyter, 1967ff), vol. 6, p. 66.

2

On Truths and Lies in an Extramoral Sense
1873

Written in 1873, but not published until thirty years later, "On Truths and Lies in an Extramoral Sense" provides a clear statement of Nietz-sche's views on consciousness and language. In particular, Nietzsche develops the thesis that language provides only a simplified, reduced, and

Translated from Friedrich Nietzsche, "Über Wahrheit und Lüge im aussermoralischen Sinne," in Nietzsche, *Werke: Kritische Gesamtausgabe*, Giorgio Colli and Mazzino Montinari, eds. (Berlin: De Gruyter, 1973), vol. 3, part 2, pp. 366–84.

therefore erroneous translation of reality because it relies on general concepts that cannot register all variation and difference. Over time, Nietzsche argues, languages became more and more set, but it was still possible to play with words, which is what Nietzsche set about doing. But play could only break the molds; it could not reveal truth. Long before Beyond Good and Evil *or* On the Genealogy of Morals, *Nietzsche was exploring the paradox that life is based on a foundation of lies, and necessarily so.*

Once upon a time, in some remote spot among the uncountable, glittering solar systems that make up the universe, there was a star on which clever animals invented knowledge. This was the most arrogant and dishonest minute in "world history," but only a single minute. After nature had drawn a few breaths, the star grew cold and the clever animals died.

You could make up such a fairy tale and still not be able to adequately describe how miserable, how shadowy and transient, how aimless and arbitrary the human intellect appears in nature. There have been eternities during which it did not exist. And when it is gone, that will be it; nothing will have changed. The fact is that the intellect has no further mission that would lead it beyond human life. It is completely human and only the human being who possesses and fashions it takes it with the seriousness that it seems to be the axis the world turns on. If we could communicate with the mosquito, we would learn that it floats through the air with the same self-importance and feels itself also to be the floating center of the universe. There is nothing in nature that is so despicable or insignificant not to immediately swell up like a balloon with the slightest puff of this power of knowledge; and just as every laborer wants to have an admirer, so even the proudest of men, the philosopher, assumes that from every direction the eyes of the universe have trained their telescopes on his actions and his thoughts.

It is curious that the intellect makes this assumption, since it was only given to the most unfortunate, fragile, and ephemeral beings as a means to catch them for a minute in existence. Without this one extra thing thrown in, they would have fled existence at the first opportunity. The arrogance that goes with knowing and sensing covers the eyes and senses like a blinding fog, deceiving them about the value of existence by providing the most flattering estimation of the value of knowledge. [. . .]

The intellect, as a means for preserving the individual, reveals its principal powers in make-believe. This is how weaker, less robust, individuals protect themselves, since they are not able to wage the struggle for existence with the horns and sharp teeth of beasts of prey. This art of simulation is most fully developed in man. Deception, flattery, lying and cheating, talking behind backs, striking a pose, living in borrowed splendor, wearing masks, hiding behind convention, putting on a show for others and for ourselves, in short, constantly fluttering around the flame of vanity, is so much the rule that nothing is more improbable than the appearance of a plain, honest desire for truth among men. They are deeply immersed in illusions and dream images; their eyes simply glide over the surface of things and see "forms." Their senses do not lead them to the truth, but simply receive stimulations and somewhat comically grope their way along the back of things. And more: man lets himself be lied to by dreams every night of his life without his sense of morality ever trying to prevent this, even when there are said to be men who have stopped snoring through sheer force of will. [. . .] In view of all this, where is there room for the desire for truth?

Insofar as the individual wants to protect himself against other individuals, he will under natural circumstances use his intellect mostly for simulation. However, at the same time, out of boredom and out of need, man wants to live socially and with the herd; he needs to make peace with others and endeavors to put an end to at least the most flagrant aspects of the "war of all against all." The peace pact that ensues even brings what looks like the first steps toward the attainment of that puzzling desire for truth. It is at this point that whatever shall be truth for the time being is fixed; that is, a uniformly valid and binding designation is invented for things and this legislative act of language furnishes the first laws of truth. For the first time, it is possible to make a distinction between what is true and what is false. The liar is the man who uses words—the valid designations—to make something unreal appear real. For example, he might say, "I am rich" when the proper designation of his situation would be the word "poor." He misuses established conventions by arbitrary changes or by switching designations. If he does this in a self-serving way that causes damage to others, he will no longer be trusted and he will be excluded from society. What men do when they exclude the liar is avoid not so much the lie but the harmful consequences of the lie. [. . .] It is much the same way with the truth. Man desires not so much truth but the pleasant, life-preserving consequences of truth. He is indifferent to pure knowledge if it has no consequences and he is outrightly hostile to pure truth that is potentially harmful and destructive. In any case, what about the conventions of language? Are they really products of knowledge, of the search for truth? Do designations correspond to things? Is language the adequate expression of all reality?

Only through forgetfulness can man ever achieve the illusion of possessing truth in the sense discussed above. If he is not content with truth in the form of tautology[1]—that is, with empty shells—then he will always exchange truths for illusions. What is a word? It is the representation of a nerve stimulus in sound. But to infer from the nerve stimulus an external cause is the false and unjustified application of the principle of reason. If the genesis of language had been determined by truth alone, if the factor of certainty had been decisive in making designations, how could we still say "the stone is hard," as if "hardness" was something we were all familiar with and was not a completely subjective stimulation! We separate things according to gender, designating the tree [*der* Baum] as masculine and the plant [*die* Pflanze] as feminine.[2] What arbitrary assignments! [. . .] We refer to a snake, a designation that refers only to its ability to coil and therefore it could also apply to a worm. What arbitrary differentiations! [. . .] Placed side by side, the various languages reveal that words are not a matter of truth or of the right expression, otherwise there would not be so many languages. The "thing in itself" (for that is what pure truth, whatever the consequences, would be) is quite incomprehensible to the creators of language and is not in the least worth attaining. For language designates things in relation to men and does so by means of the boldest metaphors. A nerve stimulus is first transposed into an image!—first metaphor, and the image, imitated by sound!—second metaphor [. . .] metaphors which in no way correspond to the original entities. [. . .]

Let us consider further the formation of concepts. Any word immediately becomes a concept when it does not serve as a reminder of the unique and wholly individual original experience to which it owes its origin, but rather must fit countless more or less similar cases, which means, strictly speaking, cases that are never equal and thus altogether unequal. Every concept is generated by equating unequal

---

[1]*tautology*: Redundant at best, misleading at worst, a tautology is a proposition that by its definition is necessarily true.

[2]*der Baum/die Pflanze*: All nouns in the German language are regarded as either masculine, feminine, or neutral.

things. Since no leaf is totally the same as another, the concept "leaf" is formed by arbitrarily discarding the individual differences among leaves, and by forgetting the distinguishing aspects, thus giving rise to the idea that in nature there might be something in addition to leaves which would be "leaf": the original model after which all leaves were woven, sketched, copied, coored, curled, and painted, but in such an incompetent way that no copy turned out to be a correct, trustworthy likeness of the original form. [...]

So, what, then, is truth? It is a mobile army of metaphors, metonyms, and anthropomorphisms—in short, a sum of human relations, which have been enhanced, transposed, and embellished in poetry and rhetoric and which, after long use, seem fixed, canonical, and binding to a people. Truths are illusions which we have forgotten are illusions. They are metaphors which have become worn out and no longer have the power to carry meaning. They are coins that have lost their images and are now considered metal and no longer as coins. We still do not know where the desire for truth comes from, for we have only considered the obligation to be truthful that society imposes on itself in order to exist, that is, the obligation to make use of the customary metaphors and, in a moral sense, to lie according to established conventions, to lie collectively in a manner binding for everyone. [...]

3

On the Uses and Disadvantages of History for Life
1874

Written in 1873 and published the next year as part of Nietzsche's Untimely Meditations, *which appeared between 1873 and 1876, "On the Uses and Disadvantages of History for Life" provides clear ideas on how history helps and hinders societies as well as individuals. In these*

Translated from Friedrich Nietzsche, "Vom Nutzen und Nachtheil der Histories für das Leben," in *Unzeitmässige Betrachtungen*, Kritische Studienausgabe, Giorgio Colli and Mazzino Montinari, eds. (Berlin: De Gruyter, 1967ff), vol. 1, pp. 245–85.

excerpts, Nietzsche distinguishes three kinds of history: monumental, antiquarian, and critical. All distort the historical record, but each also provides society with different perspectives that in combination encourage new bursts of creativity that transform rather than reproduce society. Throughout, Nietzsche is concerned with enhancing what he calls the "plastic power" of culture, the ability to give social and cultural form to chaos, just as a story provides a plot with a beginning and an end. This ability to create traditions and to tell stories, and to do so endlessly, is the singular attribute of human beings. Whether or not people will invent new traditions and come up with new stories is another matter, which is why monumental history is so important to Nietzsche. It honors the fact that there were great actions and cultural unities in the past and thus reminds people that greatness is still possible. However, antiquarian history is necessary for a people to achieve a sense of belonging, and critical history is needed to renovate a society that has become corrupt and inactive.

Foreword

"In any case, I hate everything that merely instructs me without augmenting or directly invigorating my activity." With these words from Goethe,[1] and with a sincere *ceterum censeo* ["but I am of the opinion"], our reflections on the worth and worthlessness of history may begin. It is my intention to demonstrate why instruction without invigoration, why knowledge unaccompanied by action, why history as an extravagant intellectual excess and luxury should arouse, to follow Goethe's words, our intense hatred. We still lack the essentials and what is superfluous is the enemy of what is necessary. To be sure, we need history, but not in the way that the self-indulgent idler in the garden of knowledge, looking down in his refined way upon our coarse and ungraceful needs, does. We need history for life and action, not as a pleasant diversion from life and action or as a gloss over a selfish life and a weak, cowardly action. We want to serve history only to the extent that history serves life. But the study of history can also lead to the point where life becomes stunted and degraded, a strange phenomenon of our age which is as essential as it is painful to acknowledge. [. . .]

---

[1] *Goethe*: Johann Wolfgang von Goethe (1749–1832), regarded in Nietzsche's time, as well as in our own, as one of Germany's towering literary figures.

These reflections are untimely as well because I see the pride that our era rightly takes in having a sense of history as something damaging, paralyzing, and deficient. And because I believe that we are all suffering from a consuming fever of history and we should at least recognize that we are suffering from it. But if Goethe was right to have pointed out that when we cultivate our virtues, we also add to our vices and if, as everybody knows, too much virtue—as the historical sensibility of our age seems to me to be—can ruin a people as surely as too much vice, then hear me out just this once.

1

Consider the cattle grazing before you; they do not know what is meant by yesterday or today. They jump about, eat, rest, digest, and jump about again, from morning until night, day after day. With their pleasures and displeasures, they are closely tied to the moment and are therefore neither melancholy nor bored. This is a hard sight for man to see because while he thinks himself better than the animals because he is human, he cannot help but envy them their happiness. What man wants most of all is to live like the animals, without boredom or melancholy. Yet he does so in vain because he refuses to be like them. A man may ask an animal: "Why are you just staring at me instead of telling me about your happiness?" The animal would like to reply: "The reason is because I always forget what I was going to say." But then it forgets even this answer and says nothing, so that the man was left wondering.

He wonders about himself, too, wonders that he is not able to learn how to forget but instead always clings to the past. No matter how far or how fast he runs, this chain runs with him. It is amazing: the moment was just here, now it is gone in a flash; nothing before, and nothing after, nonetheless it returns as a ghost and disturbs the peace of a later moment. Again and again, a leaf flutters from the scroll of time, falls out, floats away—and suddenly floats back again and falls in man's lap. Then the man says, "I remember," and envies the animal, who immediately forgets and watches each moment really die, as it sinks back in night and fog, forever extinguished. Thus, the animal lives *unhistorically* because it merges completely into the present, like a number that leaves no remainder. It does not know how to pretend, it hides nothing, and appears at every moment to be completely what it is, and therefore cannot be anything else but honest. Man, by contrast, struggles under the great and ever increasing weight of the past, which pushes him down and bends him sideways, encumbering his way like a dark, invisible burden. For the sake of appearances, he disowns this burden; in the company of his fellow men, he will all too happily do so, in order to arouse their envy. That is why the sight of herds grazing or, closer to him, a child who does not yet have a past to disavow and thus plays in blissful blindness between the past and the future, moves him deeply as if he had glimpsed a lost paradise. And yet the child's play will have to be disturbed. All too soon it will be called out of its forgetfulness. Then it will learn the phrase "it was," the password that brings conflict, suffering, and boredom to man, reminding him what his existence fundamentally is—a never completed past tense. If death at last brings the forgetting he longs for, it does so by extinguishing the present and all existence and by confirming his realization that existence only amounts to an uninterrupted "once was," something that lives only by negating, tearing at, and contradicting itself.

[...] The smallest happiness persisting without interruption and making us happy is infinitely more happiness than the greatest happiness which comes and goes, like a mood that lifts up for a moment in the midst of great unhappiness, longing, and privation. But in the smallest or the greatest happiness, there is always one thing that makes happiness happiness: the ability to forget or, to put it in more scholarly fashion, the capacity to feel unhistorically. The man who cannot forget all the things that have passed and pause at the threshold of the moment, who cannot stand still like the goddess of victory without feeling dizzy or frightened, will never know happiness and, even worse, will never do anything to make others happy. Imagine, in the most extreme example, the man who does not possess the strength to forget, who is doomed to see "becoming" everywhere. Such a man no longer believes in his own being, no longer believes in himself; he sees everything disintegrating into turbulent particles, and so he loses himself in the stream of becoming. As the true student of Heraclitus,[2] he will in the end hardly dare to lift a finger. All action requires forgetting, just as all living things require darkness as well as light. A man who wants to live an utterly historical existence would be like a man forced to go without sleep. [...] Therefore, while it is possible to live almost without memory, as the animals show us, it is completely impossible to live completely without forgetting. Or, to state my thesis

---

[2]*Heraclitus*: Heraclitus was an ancient Greek philosopher in the sixth century BCE whose fragmentary writings developed a philosophy of eternal, restless change that influenced Nietzsche.

even more simply: *There is a point at which sleeplessness, rumination, the historical sensibility is harmful and ultimately fatal to living things, whether a man, a people, or a culture.*

To determine this point and thereby the boundary beyond which the past must be forgotten if it is not to bury the present, we would need to know exactly how great is the *plastic power* of a man, a people, or a culture, that is, the capacity to develop out of ourselves in our own ways, to reconfigure and incorporate into ourselves what is past and what is strange, to heal wounds, to replace what is lost, to recreate broken forms. There are men who have so little of this capacity that they bleed to death from a single experience, a single painful event, or merely from a slight injustice, a scratch really. And there are other men for whom the most violent and dreadful disasters and even their own truly wicked acts mean so little that they are able to compose themselves quite quickly and come to possess a kind of clear conscience. The more strongly rooted that a man's inner nature is, the better he will be able to incorporate or expropriate the things of the past; and the most powerful and formidable man would be characterized by the absence of any boundary at which his historical sensibility would begin to overwhelm and injure him; he would draw to himself and incorporate into himself the entire past, all that is familiar and strange, and transform them into his blood. What such a man cannot master, he knows how to forget; it is not there anymore, the horizon is completely rounded off. Nothing is left to remind him that beyond this horizon there are still men, passions, teachings, and goals. It is a general law that every living thing can be healthy, strong, and fruitful only when bounded by a horizon; if it is incapable of drawing a horizon around itself or if it is too self-centered to enclose its vision inside another horizon, then it will waste away and, pale and weary, die prematurely. Good cheer, good conscience, joyful action, confidence in the future—all these depend, in the case of the individual or the collective, on the existence of a line that separates what is discernible and bright from what is unobservable and dark, on the capacity at the right moment to forget as well as to remember, on the possession of a fine instinct to determine when it is necessary to feel historically or unhistorically. This precisely is the proposition that the reader is invited to consider: *The historical and the unhistorical are necessary in equal measure for the well-being of a single individual, of a people, and of a culture.*

[...] A man's sense and knowledge of history can be very limited, his horizon hemmed in like an Alpine valley, all his judgments may be unjust, and his experiences erroneously regarded as original—but in spite of this injustice and this error he stands there superlatively healthy and vigorous and is a delight to behold; while next to him stands a man who is far more just and learned, but grows ill and collapses because the lines of the horizon are restlessly shifting, because he cannot extricate himself out of his finely woven net of truth and justice to undertake simple acts of desire and will. By contrast, we observed the animal which is completely unhistorical and lives within a horizon reduced almost to a single point, and yet is happy, or at least lives without boredom or pretense. Thus, we must conclude that the capacity to be unhistorical to a certain degree is more important and fundamental since it provides the only basis on which any sound, healthy, great, or genuinely human enterprise can develop. The unhistorical is that all-enveloping atmosphere necessary for the generation of any living thing, which would only disappear again with the destruction of this atmosphere. To be sure, man becomes man only because he imposes limits on his unhistorical element by thinking, reflecting, comparing, and distinguishing and drawing conclusions, because a vivid beam of light breaks through the all-encompassing haze, because he is able to make the past useful to life and to transform occurrences into history. But with too much history, man once again ceases to exist and without the envelope of the unhistorical he would never have begun or have dared to begin. What endeavor would man have undertaken had he not first found himself in the haze of the unhistorical? Or, to put aside this imagery and introduce an example, imagine a man seized by a violent passion for a woman or a powerful idea. How different his world has become! [. . .] All his value judgments are transformed and devalued. There are so many things he can no longer appreciate because he can hardly feel them any more. He asks himself why he simply mouthed the phrases and opinions of others for so long. He is surprised that his memory goes around and around in an endless circle, but he is too tired and weak to take even a single leap out of it. His is the most undeserved condition in the world, narrow-minded, unheedful of the past, blind to danger, deaf to any warning, a lively little whirl in a dead sea of night and oblivion. And yet this condition—unhistorical, antihistorical through and through—is the point of origin of any just or unjust action. No artist would ever paint a picture, no general win a victory, no people attain its freedom without first having desired and struggled for it in such an unhistorical condition. Just as the protagonist is always without a conscience, to use Goethe's expression, so he is also without knowledge. He forgets almost everything in order to accomplish just one thing; he is unjust toward what lies behind him and recognizes only one truth: what must be done now. Thus, the protagonist loves his deed far more than it deserves to be loved. The finest deeds take place in such an exuberance of love that they will have to remain unworthy of that love, however great they may be in other respects.

[...] Our understanding of the historical may be simply a Western prejudice, but let us make progress within this prejudice and not stand still! If only we would just learn to employ history for the purpose of *life*! [...]

A historical phenomenon which is clearly and completely understood, and which is reduced to an object of knowledge, is dead to the person who perceives it, precisely because he has perceived and noted the madness, the injustice, the blind passion, and generally the dark, dismal horizon of this phenomenon and, at the same time, recognized its power in history. This power has become powerless for the man of knowledge, but perhaps not for the man of life.

History conceived as pure scholarship and regarded as its own sovereign discipline would be a kind of settling of accounts with life, a general conclusion for mankind. Only in the service of a powerful new stream of life—of a new, emerging culture, for example—is historical knowledge something beneficial and promising for the future. Therefore, history must be dominated and directed by a higher force and must not itself dominate and direct.

Insofar as history serves life, it serves an unhistorical power and, in this subordinate role, will and should never become pure knowledge like mathematics. The question of the degree to which life even requires the service of history is one of the most important questions and concerns with regard to the well-being of a man, a people, or a culture. For when there is too much history, life crumbles and degenerates, and, finally, so does history itself.

2

That life requires the service of history has to be understood as clearly as the proposition, which will be demonstrated later, that too much history is harmful to the living. History is relevant to the living in three respects: it is useful to the man who acts and strives, to the man who preserves and venerates, and to the man who suffers and seeks deliverance. These three relationships correspond to three modes of history: to the extent that they can be distinguished, there is a *monumental*, an *antiquarian*, and a *critical* mode.

History is especially useful to the man who is active and powerful, who fights the great fight, who needs models, teachers, and comforters and who, in the present, is unable to find them among his contemporaries. [. . .] It is the man of action whom Polybius[3] has in mind when he calls political history the proper preparation for governing a state and the incomparable teacher who, by reminding us of the misfortunes of others, admonishes us to resolutely endure our own reversals of fortune. The man who has learned to recognize the meaning of history in this way will be appalled to see inquisitive tourists or pedantic micrologists scampering about the pyramids of past greatness. Here where he finds inspiration to emulate or surpass greatness, he does not want to encounter the dilettante, in quest of amusement or excitement, who saunters through history as though it was some gallery of priceless paintings. [. . .] He takes as his command: anything in the past that was able to enhance the concept "man" and make it more beautiful must always be available in order to perpetually do so again. That the great moments in the struggle of individuals constitute a chain, in which the mountaintops of humanity are joined over thousands of years so that the summit of such long-lost moments might still be alive, bright and great, for me—that is the fundamental idea of the belief in humanity expressed in the demand for a *monumental* history. But precisely this demand—that greatness shall be everlasting—incites the most dreadful struggle. Every other living man cries No. There should be nothing monumental—that is the slogan of the naysayers. Lifeless, trivial, and vulgar customs take up every corner of the world and blur everything great in a heavy fog. They clutter the path greatness must take on its way to immortality, hindering it, deceiving it, suffocating it, stifling it. And this path leads through human brains! Through the brains of frightened and short-lived animals who reappear again and again with the same ailments in a desperate struggle to postpone their destruction for a little while. [. . .] Yet again and again there are a few who do wake up and, gaining strength at the sight of past greatness, are inspired by the feeling that life is a glorious thing. The best fruit of the bitter plant of life is the knowledge that in earlier times someone lived his life with pride and strength, that another did so profoundly, and that a third did so with compassion and a helping hand, all of them leaving behind the same

---

[3]*Polybius*: Writing in the second century BCE, Polybius was originally Greek but came to be one of the great historians of ancient Rome.

lesson: that man lives best when he does not worry about his existence. If the common man takes his little span of life with morbid, greedy seriousness, the great men on the path to immortality and to monumental history regarded theirs with Olympian laughter or at least with exquisite scorn; they often went to their graves with an ironic smile. [. . .] But one thing survives: the signature of their fundamental being, a work, a deed, a rare insight, a creation; it will live because posterity cannot do without it. [. . .]

So what use to someone today is the monumental conception of the past, the engagement with the classics and the treasures of earlier times? He learns from it that greatness was at least *possible* once and therefore might be possible again; he now has a spring in his step, for the doubts which had assailed him in weaker moments, that he was perhaps desiring the impossible, have been banished. If someone believed that it would not take more than one hundred men, educated and active working in a new spirit, to do away with what has become a culture of the merely fashionable in Germany today, imagine how greatly he would be encouraged to know that the culture of the Renaissance was lifted up on the shoulders of just such a band of one hundred men.

And yet—to learn something new right away from this example—how blurred and indeterminate, how inexact the comparison would have to be! Think of all the different details of the past that would have to be overlooked for the comparison to produce its powerful effect! Think of how violently the unique aspects of the past would have to be crammed into a general form and all the sharp corners and angles broken off for the sake of consistency! In the end [. . .] monumental history will always take what is different and approximate it by endlessly generalizing and making things correspond, will always diminish the differences of motive and circumstance in order to present the *effects* as monumental—something exemplary and worthy of emulation—at the expense of the *causes*. Since monumental history ignores causes as much as possible, it is hardly an exaggeration to call it a collection of "effects in themselves," of events that will produce an effect for all times. What popular festivals and religious and military anniversaries celebrate is really just such an "effect in itself." This is what will not let the ambitious rest; this is what the brave wear over their hearts as an amulet; but this is not the truly historical interconnection between cause and effect, which, if completely understood, would only prove that the game of dice that future and chance play can never reproduce something exactly the same.

As long as the soul of historiography lies in the great *stimulation* that a man of power derives from it; as long as the past has to be described as worthy of emulation, as something that can be emulated and is possible for a second time, history is in danger of becoming so distorted and reworked into something so beautiful that it looks more like the free forms of poetry. Indeed, there have been ages which could not distinguish between a monumental past and a fictional myth, because precisely the same stimulation can be derived from one world as from the other. If the monumental consideration of history *prevails* over the antiquarian or the critical, then the past itself is *damaged*; whole segments of the past are neglected, forgotten, and washed away in an endless, colorless tide, and only a few decorative facts stand out like islands. [...] Monumental history deceives by analogies: with seductive resemblances it provokes the brave to foolhardiness and the enthusiastic to fanaticism. We can well imagine what would happen with this sort of history in the hands and heads of gifted egoists or fiery malcontents—empires would be destroyed, princes murdered, revolutions incited, and the number of historical "effects in themselves," which is to say actions without sufficient cause, constantly augmented. So much for a reminder of the damage that monumental history can do in the hands of men of power and achievement, whether they are good or evil; just think of what it could do in the hands of the powerless and inert!

Well, let us take the most simple and common example. Think of people without any artistic sense armed and emboldened by a monumental history of art. Against whom will they turn their weapons! Against their archenemies, the strong artistic spirits, that is to say, against the only ones who are able to learn from this history in a genuine, that is, life-enhancing way, and who are able to apply what they have learned to higher purposes. For these spirits, their way will be obstructed and their air darkened. When the people dance reverentially, zealously around a half-understood monument to some great past, it is as though they wanted to say: "Look, this is true art; those out there who are striving and becoming do not matter!" Obviously, this dancing mob would have the privilege of possessing "good taste," since the creative man is always at a disadvantage compared to the dilettante who merely looks on and does not take part, just as the beer-hall politician has always been more clever, more fair, and more careful than the statesman who actually rules. [...] Their instincts tell them that art can be killed by art: the monumental is never to reappear and to make sure it does not, the people invoke the authority that the monumental has acquired from the past. They are connoisseurs of art precisely in order to get rid of art. [...] They do not want to see greatness emerge, and so they say, "Look, greatness already exists!" In fact, they care as little about the greatness that already exists as they do about the greatness that might emerge; their lives are testimony to that. In their hands, monumental history is the masquerade in which their hatred for the powerful and great of their own age is disguised as bloated admiration for the powerful and great of past ages. Thereby they invert the real meaning of this historical viewpoint into its opposite. Whether they are aware of it or not, they act as though their motto were: let the dead bury the living.

Each of the three modes of history is appropriate to its own soil and its own climate. Anywhere else, each would grow into a destructive weed. If the man who wants to create any great thing needs the past at all, then he will appropriate it by means of monumental history; by contrast, the man who wants to remain alongside what is familiar and has stood the test of time will cherish the past as an antiquarian historian; and only the man who, weighed down by the adversities of his time, wants to throw off his burden at any cost, needs critical history, a history that will judge and condemn. To transplant thoughtlessly these historical growths will cause a great deal of damage: the critic would be without adversity, the antiquarian without piety, the man in awe of the greatness without the abilities of the great—these are the growths that lacking their own nurturing soil have degenerated into weeds.

3

Second, history is relevant to the man who preserves and venerates, who looks back with loyalty and love at the place where he came from, the place which made him. With this piety he gives thanks to his existence. Looking after the old formations of the past with a loving hand, he hopes to preserve the conditions under which he grew up for those who will follow him, and thus he serves life. In such a soul, the possession of the household goods of his forefathers changes its meaning: *they* rather possess *him*. All the small and trivial things, crumbling and obsolete, acquire worth and integrity when the preserving, honoring spirit of the antiquarian man settles over these things and makes them its home and nest. His city's history becomes for him his own autobiography. He reads the walls of the city, its towered gate, its laws, and its holidays like the illustrated diary of youth and he rediscovers himself in all this, his strength, his industry, his joy, his judgment, his folly, and his vices. Here men could live, he tells himself, since men live here now. And men will be able to live here in the future because we are tough and cannot be broken overnight. With this "we," he looks beyond his own transitory individual existence and feels himself to be the spirit of his house, his generation, his city. Across the long dark centuries of confusion, he greets the soul of his people as his own soul. An ability to feel his way back and sense how things were, to detect traces that have been almost extinguished, to instinctively make a correct reading of the past that has been written over many times, to quickly understand the palimpsests—these are his talents and virtues. [. . .] It was this sensibility that animated the Italians of the Renaissance and reawoke in their poets the genius of ancient Italy to the "marvelous new resounding of the ancient lyre," as Jacob Burckhardt put it.[4] But the antiquarian sense of veneration of the past is of the greatest value when it endows the modest, harsh, even impoverished conditions in which a man or a people live with a simple feeling of pleasure and satisfaction; with remarkable candor, Niebuhr,[5] for example, admits that he could live happily on moors and heaths among free peasants who possessed history; he would not miss art. How could history better serve life than to attach even less-favored people to their native homes and native customs, settling them in one place, and keeping them from roaming around looking for and then fighting for something better in strange lands? Sometimes it appears to be sheer stubbornness and stupidity for an individual to cling to his companions and his region, to his arduous routines, to his barren mountain ridges—but it is a stupidity of the most beneficial, socially useful kind. This is clear to anyone who has seen the terrible aftermath of that adventurous spirit which sometimes takes hold of entire nations or who has seen up close the condition of a people who have lost faith in their own prehistory and succumbed to a restless cosmopolitan craving for new and ever more new things. The opposite feeling, the satisfaction of the tree in its own roots, the happiness to know that we are not a completely arbitrary or accidental creation, but have grown out of a past to which we are heir, blossom, and fruit, and thus

---

[4]Jacob Burckhardt, *The Civilization of the Renaissance in Italy*, trans. S. G. C. Middlemore (Oxford: Phaidon Press, 1945), p. 153; originally *Kultur der Renaissance in Italien: Ein Versuch* (Basel: Schweighauser, 1860).

[5]*Niebuhr.* Barthold Georg Niebuhr (1776–1831), a Danish-born historian who taught in Berlin and published a major history of ancient Rome.

to know that our existence is excused, indeed justified—this is what I would call a real sense of history.

Of course, these are not the conditions that would best enable a man to reduce the past to pure scholarship; so here we perceive, as we have for monumental history, that the past itself suffers as long as history serves life and is governed by the impulses of life. Or, to put it more metaphorically, a tree is more able to feel its roots than see them, but it measures their size by the extent and strength of the branches that it can see. Now, if a tree could be wrong about its own roots, how much more wrong it would be about the whole forest around it! It knows the forest only for what the forest might do for the tree—and nothing more. The antiquarian sensibility of a man, or a neighborhood, or an entire people will always have an extremely restricted field of vision; it simply does not take notice of most things, and the little that it does see, it sees in isolation and much too closely; it cannot measure anything and therefore gives everything equal importance, and thus each single thing too much importance. There is no criterion of value or sense of proportion that would sort out the things of the past in a way that would do them justice, only the measure of the antiquarian man looking backward.

The danger in this is close at hand. Everything that is seen as old and past will ultimately be regarded as equally venerable, while everything that does not treat the past with reverence, that is, everything new and emerging, is rejected and condemned. [. . .] When the sensibility of a people hardens in this way, when history serves the life of the past so that it undermines those living and striving, when the historical sense no longer conserves life, but embalms it, then the tree dies prematurely, withering gradually from the top down to the roots until the roots themselves perish. The moment antiquarian history is no longer animated and enlivened by the fresh life of the present, it degenerates. Its piety withers away, while the habit of scholarship continues on, revolving complacently around its own center. Then what we see is the repulsive spectacle of a blind mania for collecting things, a relentless raking together of everything that has ever existed. Man envelopes himself in mustiness. His antiquarian ways have succeeded in reducing what was a valuable attachment and a noble desire into a voracious appetite for novelty, that is for antiquity, for everything. There are many cases when he finally sinks so low that he is satisfied with any fare and happily gobbles down the dust of bibliographical minutiae.

Even if this degeneration does not occur [. . .] the danger remains that antiquarian history will become too powerful and overwhelm the other modes of regarding the past. It knows only how to *preserve* life, not to create life. For that reason, it persistently undervalues becoming because it lacks the instinctive feel for it, which is something that monumental history, for example, does have. Thus, antiquarian history impedes the firm resolve to attempt something new; it paralyzes the man of action, who, as one who acts, necessarily will offend some piety or another. The fact that things have become old now leads to the demand that they be made immortal. For if we add up all the experiences that such things—an old ancestral custom, a religious belief, an inherited political privilege—have acquired over the course of their existence, and the sum total of the piety and veneration with which individuals and generations have endowed them, then it seems presumptuous and even cruel to replace such antiquity with novelty and to set such a huge quantity of piety and honor against the single unit of what is becoming and making itself present.

Now it will become clear how necessary it is for man to have, in addition to the monumental and antiquarian modes to regard the past, a *third*, the *critical*, which also stands in the service of life. In order to live, man must possess the strength and, from time to time, employ it to break up and dissolve the past. He achieves this by bringing the past before a tribunal, interrogating it closely, and finally condemning it. Every past deserves to be condemned—for that is the nature of all things human. They have always shown a capacity for violence and weakness. It is not justice that sits in judgment here; even less is it mercy that pronounces the verdict: it is life alone, the dark, driving, greedily self-desiring power. Its verdicts are always unmerciful, always unjust, because they never flow from a pure fountain of knowledge. But in most cases justice itself would pronounce the same verdict, "since all that gains existence, is only fit to be destroyed, that's why it would be best if nothing ever got created."[6] It takes a great deal of strength to live and to forget the degree to which life and injustice are one and the same thing. [. . .] But from time to time, the same life that requires forgetting demands its suspension in order for it to become clear just how wrong the existence of a privilege, a caste, or a dynasty is and just how thoroughly it deserves to perish. Then one will exam-

---

[6]Johann Wolfgang von Goethe, *Faust 1 & 2*, Stuart Atkins, ed. and trans. (Princeton, N.J.: Princeton University Press, 1994), p. 36 (part 1, lines 1339–41).

ine the past critically, taking a knife to its roots and cruelly trampling over any and all pieties. The undertaking is always dangerous, dangerous for life. And men and ages which serve life by judging and destroying a past are always dangerous and endangered. For since we are the products of previous generations, we are also the products of their blunders, passions, and mistakes, even of their crimes; it is not possible to free ourselves completely from this chain. When we condemn these mistakes and consider ourselves free of them, the fact remains that we originated from them. The best we can do is to create a conflict between our inherited ancestral nature and our knowledge, and to bring a new, stern discipline into combat with our inborn, inbred heritage. We cultivate in ourselves a new habit, a new instinct, a second nature so that the first nature will wither away. It is an attempt to give ourselves a past, as it were a posteriori, a past from which we would have liked to originate in opposition to the past from which we did originate—always a dangerous undertaking since it is difficult to set limits to this rejection of the past and because second natures are usually weaker than first natures. What happens all too often is that we recognize what is good but fail to do it, because we also know what is better and fail to do that. Here and there we achieve a victory, and for those who struggle, who know how to use critical history to serve life, there is an important consolation: namely, the knowledge that this first nature was once a second nature and that every victorious second nature will become a first.

5

In five respects, it seems to me, too much history is hostile and dangerous to life. Too much history creates the contrast between inner and outer life and thereby weakens the personality; too much history induces an age to imagine that it possesses, to a greater degree than any other age, the most treasured of virtues, justice; too much history disrupts the instincts of the people and hinders both the individual and the collective from maturing; too much history sows the seeds of the belief, harmful at any time, that mankind has grown old, the belief that we are latecomers and epigones; too much history puts an age into the dangerous attitude of irony about itself and subsequently into the even more dangerous state of cynicism: the age develops in an ever more clever and egoistic fashion, which paralyzes and finally destroys the forces of life.

4

Human, All Too Human
1878

Published in 1878, this selection is part of a sprawling collection of apho-
risms and insights into religion, law, social convention, and human rela-
tions. Many of the aphorisms that appear in Document 1 are drawn
from Human, All Too Human. *This excerpt is particularly useful because*
it expresses Nietzsche's ideas about national identity and cultural authen-
ticity. It also reveals both Nietzsche's typical brittleness about Jews and
his even greater scorn for anti-Semites. In the end, Nietzsche declares
himself to be a "good European" because he repudiates the loyalties of
nationalism, which at one point he called "soil addiction." [1] *Any argu-*
ment that puts Nietzsche in the service of German nationalism or
Nazism has to contend with this text.

Section 475

European Man and the Destruction of Nations. Commerce and industry, the circulation of books and letters, the basic uniformity of all
higher culture, the frequent forth and back to different places and
regions, what has become a nomadic life for everyone but farmers—
these circumstances are weakening and may finally lead to the
destruction of nations, at least the European ones. As a consequence
of constant crossbreeding, a mixed race of European men will emerge.
Whether consciously or unconsciously, the European nations are
resisting the end of their existence by inflaming *national* hostilities,
but despite these temporary countercurrents, racial mixing is gradually proceeding. In any case, this artificial nationalism is as dangerous
as artificial Catholicism once was because, in essence, it is a state of

---

[1]Section 241, *Jenseits von Gut und Böse*, Kritische Studienausgabe, Giorgio Colli and
Mazzino Montinari, eds. (Berlin: De Gruyter, 1967ff), vol. 5, p. 180; also translated as
Beyond Good and Evil, Walter Kaufmann, trans. (New York: Random House, 1966),
p. 174.

Translated from Friedrich Nietzsche, "Ein Blick auf den Staat," *Menschliches, Allzumen-*
schliches, Kritische Studienausgabe, Giorgio Colli and Mazzino Montinari, eds. (Berlin:
De Gruyter, 1967ff), vol. 2.

emergency forcibly imposed by the few on the many and because it requires deceit, lies, and violence in order for it to be taken seriously. It is not the interests of the majority (of the people), as is no doubt claimed, but above all the interests of certain ruling dynasties and also of particular classes in industry and high society that promote this nationalism. Once you have realized this, you should simply openly declare yourself to be a *good European* and actively work to merge the nations together. The Germans, with their time-tested talent for being *interpreters and mediators between peoples* can help in this endeavor. Incidentally, the entire problem of the *Jews* only exists within national states. Their energy and higher intelligence, and the capital of will and spirit that they have accumulated in their long ordeal over the generations, have made them successful to the point that they now arouse envy and hatred, so much so that in almost every nation the vulgar journalistic practice of leading the Jews to slaughter as scapegoats for every imaginable public or private misfortune is gaining ground — more so in the more nationalistic countries. As soon as it is no longer a question of conserving the nation but of producing the strongest possible mixed race, the Jews will be as usable and desirable an ingredient in the mix as any other national residue. Every nation, every man, has unpleasant, even dangerous characteristics; it is cruel to demand that the Jews should constitute an exception. Even if the characteristics of the Jews are particularly dangerous and repulsive and even if the young Jew from the stock exchange is the most disgusting specimen of the entire human race, nonetheless, I would like to know how much, in a general accounting, we will have to forgive a people, and here we are very much to blame, who have had the most tragic history and whom we owe the most noble man (Christ), the purest wise man (Spinoza),[2] and the mightiest book and most effective moral code in the world. Moreover, in the darkest periods of the Middle Ages, when cloudbanks from Asia settled low over Europe,[3] it was Jewish freethinkers, scholars, and physicians who, under the harshest conditions, held up the banner of enlightenment and intellectual independence and defended Europe against Asia. It is thanks not least to their efforts that a more natural, rational, and generally unmythical

---

[2]*Spinoza*: Benedict de Spinoza (1632–1677). Misleadingly accused of atheism, the Dutch-born Spinoza achieved prominence as one of the foremost rationalist philosophers of his time.

[3]*when cloudbanks from Asia settled low over Europe*: Nietzsche persistently characterizes Christianity as Asian and the Middle Ages as the high point of Christian influence.

explanation of the world could finally once more prevail and that the cultural ties that bind us with the enlightenment of Graeco-Roman antiquity remain enduring. If Christianity has done everything to orientalize the West, Judaism has always played an essential part in westernizing it again: which really amounts to making Europe's task and history the *continuation of the Greek.*

5

The Gay Science
1882

Nietzsche might well have insisted on the title of this English translation since he subtitled the German original, Die fröhliche Wissenschaft, *published in 1882, with the Provencal "la gaya scienza," which referred to the "southern," Mediterranean flavor of the book. It has nothing to do with homosexuality; "gay" had different connotations in the nineteenth century. By invoking "joyous" or "cheerful" knowledge, Nietzsche wanted to be playful as well as impious, to show that the methods of science were not necessarily ponderous, and to argue against the systematic "true" organization of knowledge. Nearly four hundred entries, some quite short, make up* The Gay Science; *they do not form a coherent argument but instead represent a sustained effort to excavate beneath cherished truths. In these excerpts, Nietzsche pursues two interrelated aims. First, he discusses the "death of God" in the famous excerpt "The Madman" (section 125) in order to prompt human beings to acknowledge that they have murdered God, and thereby to gain perspective on the origin of morality, to examine hostility to new things (section 4), and to explore new ways of life in which they are not beholden to any higher power (sections 283 and 342). This will be a very difficult thing to do; already the madman approaches a state of despair: "Who will wipe the blood off? Where is the water to clean ourselves?" The ancient Greeks, however,*

Translated from Friedrich Nietzsche, *Die fröhliche Wissenschaft*, Kritische Studienausgabe, Giorgio Colli and Mazzino Montinari, eds. (Berlin: De Gruyter, 1967ff), vol. 3.

provide a historical example of life very different, in Nietzsche's view more free and more bold, from Christianity (section 143). Here he locates the origin of the "luxury" of individuality. Second, just as Nietzsche examined how moral codes created authoritative but basically unverifiable truths, he contemplates the tendentious ways in which human beings describe the universe, giving it lifelike and even human attributes and filling its emptiness with the divine (sections 109 and 121). Nietzsche knows that people need to live with familiarity and predictability (section 355), which he regards as the foundation of scientific description and the origin of language itself (section 354), but he also wants to use the "death of God" as an opportunity to live without these familiar aids, to recognize the isolated and exceptional nature of life on earth. Nietzsche works on these ideas again in "On Truths and Lies in an Extramoral Sense" (Document 2) and in Beyond Good and Evil *(Document 7, section 268). Nietzsche thus elaborates on his favorite topics of Christian morality, the Greeks, and the gods, but goes on to make provocative statements about the nature of scientific inquiry and the origins of language.*

Section 4

What Sustains Life. The strongest and most evil spirits have up to now contributed the most to advance humanity: again and again they reignited the passions that had fallen asleep—all ordered societies put the passions to sleep—again and again, they reawakened the appreciation for comparing and contrasting, an appetite for things that are new, daring, and untried; they compelled people to set opinions against opinions, ideals against ideals. They did so by force of arms usually, overturning boundary markers and violating established pieties, but also with new religions and new morals! The same "evil" is in every teacher and preacher of the *new*. [. . .] What is new is under all circumstances *evil*; it wants to conquer, to overturn boundary markers and established pieties; and only what is old is good! In any epoch, the good men are those who work old thoughts deep into the earth and get them to bear fruit, they are the tillers of the spirit. But all ground eventually becomes exhausted, and the plowshares of evil will eventually have to appear. Nowadays there is a completely wrongheaded morality that is widely celebrated in England, namely, that the judgments about "good" and "evil" arise out of collective experiences with what is "beneficial" and "not beneficial."[1] Accordingly, something is called good if it sustains life, while something is called bad if it causes injury. But in truth, evil instincts are just as beneficial, sustaining, and necessary as good ones—their purpose is just different.

Section 108

New Struggles. After Buddha died, his shadow in the cave was still shown for hundreds of years—it was an extremely gruesome shadow. God is dead, but given the way people are, there will be caves in which his shadow will be shown for perhaps thousands of years. And we—we still have his shadow to vanquish!

Section 109

Let Us Beware. Let us beware of conceiving the world as a living thing. Into what does it expand? How does it feed itself? How can it grow and propagate? We more or less know what the organic is, so how can we take the exceedingly derivative, late, scarce, chance things that we perceive only on the crust of the earth and reinterpret them as essential, universal, and eternal, as do those people who call the universe an organism? That makes me sick. Let us likewise beware of believing that the universe is a machine. It certainly is not constructed for a purpose; we give it much too much honor with the word "machine." Let us beware of generalizing from the elegant orbits of our neighboring stars. Just a glance into the Milky Way suggests that there are much more imperfect and contradictory movements, as well as stars with eternally straight trajectories, and the like. The astral order in which we live is an exception and this order and temporary duration that depends on it, in turn, made possible an exception of exceptions: the generation of organic life. By contrast, the general character of the world is, for all eternity, chaos—not in the sense of lack of necessity, but in the sense of lack of order, arrangement, form, beauty, wisdom, and what our aesthetic human characteristics are all called. On the basis of our reason, we know that the unlucky rolls of the dice are the rule, the exceptions do not constitute a secret purpose, and the whole music box endlessly plays its tune, which should never be regarded a

---

[1] *wrong-headed morality:* Nietzsche is referring to nineteenth-century utilitarianism, a system of ethics that derived the idea of good from whatever best served the greater majority.

melody. Indeed the word "unlucky roll" is itself an anthropomorphization that serves as a reproach. How can we reproach or praise the universe! Let us beware of attributing to it heartlessness and unreason or their opposites. It is neither perfect, nor beautiful, nor precious and it has no desire to become these things. It certainly does not strive to imitate human beings! It is not in the least affected by our aesthetic and moral judgments! It does not have an instinct for self-preservation or any other instinct; it knows no laws. Let us beware of saying that there are laws in nature. There are only necessities, but there is no one who commands, no one who obeys, no one who transgresses. And if you know that there are no purposes, then you also know there is no coincidence: only in a world of purpose does the word "coincidence" have meaning. Let us beware of saying that death is opposed to life. The living is only a type of what is dead, and a very rare type.—Let us beware of thinking that the world is eternally creating new things. There are no eternally durable substances; matter is just as much an error as the God of the Eleatics.[2] When will we stop being so careful and caring! When will all these shadows of God stop darkening our lives! When will we have nature without God! When will we be allowed to begin to *naturalize* human beings with a pure, newly found, newly redeemed nature?

Section 121

Life is not an Argument. We have fashioned for ourselves a world in which we can live by positing bodies, lines, planes, causes and effects, motion and rest, form and content. Without these articles of faith nobody now could endure life! But that does not prove them to be correct. Life is not an argument. The conditions of life might include error.

Section 125

The Madman. Haven't you heard of that madman, who on a bright morning day lit a lantern, ran into the marketplace, and screamed incessantly: "I am looking for God! I am looking for God!" Since there were a lot of people standing around who did not believe in God, he only aroused great laughter. Is he lost? asked one person. Did he lose

---

[2]*Eleatics*: A school of ancient Greek philosophers in southern Italy that stressed the eternal and noncontradictory makeup of the universe.

his way like a child? asked another. Or is he in hiding? Is he frightened of us? Has he gone on a journey? Or emigrated? And so they screamed and laughed. The madman leaped into the crowd and stared straight at them. "Where has God gone?" he cried. "I will tell you! *We have killed him.* You and I! All of us are his murderers! But how did we do this? How did we manage to drink up the sea? Who gave us the sponge to wipe away the entire horizon? What were we doing when we unchained this earth from its sun? Where is it going now? Where are we going? Away from all the suns? Aren't we ceaselessly falling? Backward, sideways, forward, in all directions? Is there an up or a down at all? Aren't we just roaming through an infinite nothing? Don't you feel the breath of this empty space? Hasn't it gotten colder? Isn't night and ever more night falling? Don't we have to light our lanterns in the morning? Do we hear anything yet of the noise of the gravediggers who are burying God? Do we smell anything yet of the rot of God's decomposition? Gods decompose too! God is dead! God will stay dead! And we have killed him! How do we console ourselves, the murderers of all murderers? The holiest and mightiest the world has ever known has bled to death against our knives—who will wipe the blood off? Where is the water to cleanse ourselves? What sort of rituals of atonement, what sort of sacred games, will we have to come up with now? Isn't the greatness of this deed too great for us? Don't we have to become gods ourselves simply to appear worthy of it? There has never been a greater deed, and whoever will be born after us will belong to a history greater than any history up to now!"

Section 143

The Great Benefit of Polytheism. For an individual to find his *own* ideals and derive his law, his pleasures, and his rights from them—that was considered perhaps the most monstrous of all human errors and idolatry itself; indeed, the few who have dared to do this felt necessary to offer an apology which usually goes like this: "It wasn't me! it wasn't me! it was *a god* working through me!" The wonderful art and ability to create gods—polytheism—was the way this drive could unburden itself, and cleanse, realize, and ennoble itself: for originally this was an ordinary and unremarkable drive, related to obstinacy, disobedience, and envy. This drive to deny one's own ideals was once the foundation of all custom. Then there was only one norm, *man*, and every people believed they possessed this one and only norm. But above and beyond ourselves, in a distant overworld, *any number of norms* could be seen; one god was not the negation or sacrilege of another! It was here that the luxury of individuals was first permitted; it was here that the rights of individuals were first honored. The invention of gods, heroes, and supermen of all kinds, as well as near-men and submen, dwarfs, fairies, centaurs, satyrs, demons, and devils, was the priceless first attempt to vindicate the selfhood and self-love of the individual: the freedom one granted a god against the other gods one finally took for oneself against laws, customs, and neighbors. By contrast, monotheism, the rigid doctrine that only one standard human type exists—that is, the belief in one standard god next to whom there could only be false gods—posed the greatest danger to humanity. It threatened to stop humanity short. This is the stagnation that most other animal species have attained long ago for they all believe in one standard form and ideal for their species. [. . .] Polytheism provided an example for the freespiritedness and many-spiritedness of humanity: the strength to create for ourselves our own new eyes—and ever again new eyes that are even more our own: hence man alone among all the animals has no eternal horizons or perspectives.

Section 283

Men in Preparation. I welcome all the signs that a new more masculine, more warlike age is coming, one which will above all make courage honorable again! For it should prepare the way for an even greater age and gather the strength that it will need—an age that recognizes heroism and *wages war* in the name of ideas and their implications. It will be necessary to have many heroic men who are making preparations, but they do not just come out of nothing, much less out of the sand and slime of our contemporary civilization and big-city culture; it will be necessary to have men who understand how to be silent, solitary, determined, who are content and firm in their unrecognized bravery; men who are determined to search for all those things in themselves that must be *overcome*; men who are distinguished as much by good cheer, patience, simplicity, and contempt for the great vanities as they are by generosity in victory and indulgence for the little vanities of the conquered; men who can freely and clearly judge all victors and understand the role of chance in every victory and glory; men with their own celebrations, their own working days, their own mourning periods, accustomed to command and, when necessary, ready to obey, just as proud to serve their cause doing the one as the other; men more endangered, men more creative, men more happy! Because, believe me, the secret to achieve the greatest creativity and the greatest enjoyment in existence is to *live dangerously*! Build your cities on Mt. Vesuvius![3] Send your ships to undiscovered seas! Be at war with others and yourself! Seekers of knowledge, be robbers and conquerors as long as you cannot be rulers and occupiers! The time will soon be over when you are content to live hidden in the woods like timid stags! At long last, the search for knowledge will reach out to get what it is owed—it will want to *rule* and *occupy*, as you will!

Section 285

Excelsior! "You will never again pray, never again worship, never again rest in endless trust; you do not permit yourself to stand before an ultimate wisdom, ultimate goodness, ultimate power and set down your thoughts; you do not have a perpetual guardian or friend for your seven solitudes; you live without a view of the mountains with snow on their peaks and fire in their hearts; there is no one who will avenge or improve you; there is no longer any purpose in what happens, any love in what will happen to you; there is no longer a resting place open to your heart, where it would no longer to seek, but only find; you resist any kind of ultimate peace; you want the eternal recurrence of war and peace—man of renunciation, all this you want to renounce? Who will give you the strength to do this? No one has yet had this strength!" There was a lake which one day refused to flow off and so it threw a dam where the waters used to flow. Since then, this lake has been rising higher and higher. Perhaps this very renunciation will give us the strength to bear this renunciation; perhaps man will rise higher and higher, when he no longer *flows out* into a god.

Section 324

In Mid-Life. No, life has not disappointed me! Year after year I find it much more true, desirable, and mysterious—since that day when I was liberated by the idea that life could be an experiment for the seeker of knowledge, and not a duty or a curse or a swindle. And knowledge itself: for others it is something else, a bed to rest on, for example, or the way to find such a bed, or a diversion or a form of

---

[3] *Mt. Vesuvius*: In the year 79 CE, a volcanic eruption destroyed the Roman city of Pompeii, which was built at the foot of Mount Vesuvius, near present-day Naples, Italy.

entertainment; for me it is a world of dangers and victories, in which even heroic feelings find a place to dance and play. *"Life as a means to knowledge"* —you can live not only courageously but *live happily and laugh happily* if you take this principle to your heart. And how can you understand how to laugh well and live well if you do not first know a great deal about war and victory?

Section 343

The Meaning of Our Cheerfulness. The greatest event of recent times—that "God is dead," that the belief in the Christian God has become unbelievable—has already cast its first shadows over Europe. For a few at least, whose eyes, the *suspicion* in whose eyes is strong and acute enough for this sight, a sun seems to have just set, an ancient, abiding faith turned into doubt. Every day our old world must look more like evening, more mistrustful, stranger, "older" to them. But for the most part, the event itself is far too big, too distant, too removed from the capacity of people to comprehend it for us to consider that even the news of it has been *received*. Much less do people understand *what* has actually occurred—understand all the things that must collapse now that this faith has been undermined because they were built on its foundations, rested against it, had grown into it, our entire European morality, for example. The long profusion and succession of breakdown, destruction, ruin, upheaval that is now impending—who today can make out enough of all this to be the teacher and forecaster of this monstrous logic of terrors, to be the prophet of gloom and the sun's eclipse the likes of which has probably never yet occurred on earth. Even for those of us, born puzzle solvers, who are waiting in the mountains, sitting between today and tomorrow, stretched in the contradiction between today and tomorrow, we first men, the premature births of the coming century, who *should* really by now have discerned the shadows that will soon envelope Europe—why is it that we look out at the approaching gloom without any real sense of involvement nor any worry or fear for *ourselves*? [. . .] For *us* the consequences are quite the opposite of what might be expected, certainly not tragic and gloomy, in a way a kind of indescribable light, good fortune, relief, exhilaration, encouragement, dawn. . . . Indeed, when we hear that "old God is dead," we philosophers and "free spirits" feel the light of a new dawn; our hearts overflow with gratitude, astonishment, anticipation, expectation—at long last, the horizon, even if it is not bright, appears clear to us again, at long last our ships can set out again to face any danger. All the risks of seeking knowledge are once again permissible. The sea, *our* sea, is once again open; perhaps there was never such an "open sea."

Section 354

On "the Genius of the Species." We become aware of the problem of consciousness (or rather, becoming conscious of oneself) if we begin to comprehend how we might do without it. [. . .] For we could think, feel, desire, remember, we could "act" in every sense of the word, and yet none of that would necessarily have to "enter our consciousness" (as the metaphor goes). All of life would be possible even if it never saw itself in the mirror, and in fact the vast portion of life actually does take place without this mirroring—including our thinking, feeling, desiring life—offensive as this may be to older philosophers. To *what end* consciousness if it is in large part *superfluous*?

Now it seems to me, if you are willing to listen to my answer and my perhaps extravagant assumptions, that the subtle and sharp quality to consciousness is always related to a person's (or animal's) *capacity to communicate*; which, in turn, is related to the *need to communicate.* This does not mean that the individual person who is particularly adept at communication and at making his needs known would be that much more dependent on others. But it does seem to work that way when it comes to whole races and chains of generations. Over time, need and misery have forced people to communicate with each another, to make themselves quickly and exactly understood, ultimately creating a well-developed capacity for communication, just as a fortune gradually accumulates, waiting for an heir who can squander it (so-called artists are these heirs, along with orators, preachers, writers, all the people who appear at the end of a long chain, "born late" every one of them, in the best sense of the phrase, who by their nature *squander*). If this observation is correct I can make the assumption that *consciousness has only developed under the pressure of the need to communicate*, that from the beginning it was only necessary or useful as something between people (in special cases, between rulers and ruled) and that it developed only in proportion to its usefulness. Consciousness is really only a net of relations between one person and another—only as such did it need to emerge; a man who lived in solitude beastlike would not have needed it. That our actions, thoughts, feelings, movements enter our consciousness—at least to some extent—is the result of a "must" that has made demands on human beings for a terribly long time. As the most endangered animal, man *needed* help, shelter, and his own kind, he needed to know how to express his distress and make himself understood—and for all this, he needed consciousness, that is, he needed to "know" what he lacked, to "know" how he felt, to "know" what he was thinking. To say it again, like any living creature, man is always thinking, without knowing it; thinking that has become *conscious* of itself is only the smallest part, the most superficial, the most impoverished part—for this self-conscious thinking only *occurs by means of words, that is to say, symbols of communication*, by which consciousness becomes aware of its origins. In short, the development of language and the development of consciousness (*not* of reason but rather the way reason becomes conscious of itself) go hand in hand. Moreover, there are other things besides language that serve as a bridge for communication between people: a glance, a touch, a gesture. Our consciousness of our own sensory impressions, the ability to fix them, and at the same time to convey them externally has increased in proportion to the growing need to communicate with *others* by means of signs. As human beings invent signs, they become ever more sharply conscious of themselves. It was only as a social animal that man became conscious of himself, which is still happening, more and more.

As you can see, my idea is that consciousness is not something that belongs to the individual existence of a person, but rather to his social and herd nature. It follows that the intricacies of consciousness are developed only through what is useful for the collective or the herd, and, consequently, that each one of us who makes the best effort to understand ourselves individually, "to know ourselves," succeeds only in bringing not what is individual, but what is "average" to consciousness. Our thoughts are continually made generic by the character of consciousness—by "the genius of the species" that commands it—and translated back into the perspective of the herd. All our actions are incomparably personal, unique, and completely individual, there is no doubt about that, but as soon as we translate them into consciousness *they no longer appear to be so.* . . . This is what *I* take phenomenology and perspectivism[4] to be: The nature of our *animal-like consciousness* has the effect that the world of which we can become conscious is only a surface world of signs, a generalized and degraded

[4]*phenomenology and perspectivism*: Views that refer to Nietzsche's contention that the world is only as we interpret it and so it must be simplified or downgraded in order to fit into our categories of description and interpretation.

world. Therefore, everything about which we become conscious also becomes flat, slight, dumber, general, a symbol, a signal to the herd; all consciousness is related to a comprehensive process of making things corrupt, false, superficial, and general. In the end, the growth of consciousness is a danger, and whoever lives among the most conscious Europeans knows that it is a disease. As you can guess, I am not concerned with the opposition between subject and object; this distinction I will leave to epistemologists who have become entangled in the snares of word play (the metaphysics of the people). And it is certainly not the opposition between the "thing in itself" and appearance, for we do not "know" nearly enough to make such a distinction. We simply do not have an organ for *knowledge*, for "truth": we "know" (or think we know) exactly as much as is *useful* to the interests of the human herd, the species; and even what we call "useful" is in the end a mere belief, a conceit, and perhaps that most calamitous stupidity that will in the end destroy us.

Section 355

The Origins of our Concept of "Knowledge." This example comes from the street. I heard a person say, "He knew me right away." I asked myself, what do the people actually take for knowledge? What do they want when they want "knowledge"? Nothing more than this: Something strange is to be made into something *familiar*. And we philosophers, have we taken knowledge for anything *more*? The familiar consists of what we are used to so that we do not have to wonder about it, consists of our everyday, of whatever rule we are applying, of all the things that make us feel at home. How does this work? Isn't our need for knowledge just this need for the familiar, the desire to find something that will no longer disturb us in everything that is strange, unusual, or questionable? Is it not the *instinct of fear* that prompts us to know? Isn't the satisfaction of knowing not the satisfaction of a restored sense of security? . . . The philosopher considered the world "known" once he made an idea of it; well, isn't that because the idea was so well known, so familiar? because he was no longer frightened of the idea?—How complacent are the seekers of knowledge! Just take a look at their principles and their solutions to the world's riddles! When they find something in things, under things, behind things that is completely familiar to us, a multiplication table, for example, or logic or wants and wishes, how happy they immediately are! For "what is familiar is known"—they would all agree with that. Even the more careful ones suppose that what is familiar is at least *easier to know* than what is strange and proceed with the premise that we start with the "inner world," from "facts of consciousness," because these are *more familiar to us.* Error of errors! The familiar is what we are used to, and what we are used to is the most difficult to "know," to approach as a problem, as something strange and distant, "outside ourselves." [. . .]

6

Thus Spoke Zarathustra
1883–1884

Written mostly in 1882 and 1883, Thus Spoke Zarathustra *is a rambling collection of discourses by a would-be prophet, Nietzsche's invention through which he speaks. Six of these, including parts of the longer summary, "Of Old and New Tablets," and the ten-part prologue have been selected here.* Thus Spoke Zarathustra *is both an off-putting and an accessible, funny text.*

In Zarathustra, *Nietzsche chose an unlikely character. Zarathustra is not at all part of the repertoire of Western culture but is based on the historical figure of Zoroaster, the founder of the ancient Persian religion Zoroastrianism and the author of its bible in the sixth century BCE. According to Nietzsche, Zoroaster was the first of the great prophets to propound a stern morality of good and evil, which Nietzsche's Zarathustra now urges the people to renounce. Nietzsche tried to fashion his own prophetic style with short and repetitious declarations and questions, and when he is successful,* Thus Spoke Zarathustra *reads like the strokes of the hammer with which Nietzsche imagines himself philosophizing and with which Zarathustra casts the figure of the superman.*

The prophetic style is plain in the title Thus Spoke Zarathustra *and in the "thus he spoke" refrain in the Prologue. Throughout, Nietzsche both mocked and imitated the Bible, which makes the discourses seem a bit unfocused. However,* Thus Spoke Zarathustra *is also very evocative.*

Translated from Friedrich Nietzsche, *Also Sprach Zarathustra*, Kritische Studienausgabe, Giorgio Colli and Mazzino Montinari, eds. (Berlin: De Gruyter, 1967ff), vol. 4.

Its imagery is shimmering and colorful. In reading Thus Spoke Zarathustra, *it is helpful to remember how much time Nietzsche spent writing in the Swiss Alps. So many of the portraits are Alpine: the mountains, the storms that rush in the valleys, the forests and meadows, the icy rivers and the bridges that span them, the lakes and towns below. Zarathustra and his disciples walk from place to place, as the small towns in these valleys were not far apart, and on their way, they run into all sorts of characters. It is along these mountain paths that Zarathustra offers his discourses and finds himself both repelled by the people who do not listen and attracted to the people who can become supermen. Zarathustra wants to "go under" and "go down," that is, leave the mountaintops and offer his teachings to the people. But going under also means drowning, slipping away, or perishing, which points to Nietzsche's persistent playfulness about death as a requirement for life.*

Zarathustra, like Nietzsche, is a lonely man, but he wants to go down and teach among the people in the town. In the end, he is rejected, and the deaf and dumb nature that he subsequently ascribes to human beings is a major theme in Nietzsche's texts. He becomes aware of how strongly people cling to the ideas they happen to hold as truths. But Nietzsche sticks to his purpose of sending Zarathustra off on his journeys to gather disciples and to announce the self-enhancing prospect of the superman. The superman is what man would become if he overcame what was old and dead in his life and created his own laws and set out on his own voyages and did so repeatedly. (See "A Note about the Text and Translation": Nietzsche's "superman" is translated from the German Übermensch, a superlative person who can be either a man or a woman.) This adventure in building, tearing down, and rebuilding the self, however, depends on understanding that "God is dead" and that there are no powers except those discovered and created on earth. Thus, superman is entirely worldly. Nietzsche had Zarathustra teach the theme of overcoming in many ways. It is central to the parable about the camel, the lion, and the child in "On the Three Metamorphoses"; it is repeated in the images of new and broken tablets, which recall the Ten Commandments; and it is shown in the metaphor of fire and ash, the ashes of an old life that are carried up the mountain and the fire of a new life that is carried down into the valley. Bridges are also a perfect embodiment of the journey without destination that Nietzsche commends. Life is an experiment, his Zarathustra insists, and truth is the knowledge that this is possible and that all life forms are just these experiments. In this regard, Zarathustra is not only smashing tablets, but also promoting new laws and new ways of being and responding to every No with a new Yes.

PROLOGUE

1

When Zarathustra was thirty years old he left his home and the lake by his home and went into the mountains. Here he enjoyed his spirit and his solitude and for ten years he did not grow tired. But at last he had a change of heart, and one morning he woke at dawn, stood before the sun, and thus spoke Zarathustra:

Great star! Could you be happy if you did not have those for whom you shine!

For ten years you have come up here to my cave; you would have grown tired of your light and of your journey had it not been for me, my eagle, and my serpent.

We waited for you every morning, took your overflow from you, and blessed you.

But look! I am sick of my wisdom, like the bee that has gathered too much honey; I need outstretched hands to hold it.

I want to give it away and hand it out until the wise men among us are once again happy with their folly and the poor with their riches.

To do that I must climb down into the depths, as you do in the evening when you go behind the sea and bring light to the underworld, you superabundant star!

Like you, I have to *go down*, as the men to whom I want to descend put it.

So bless me then, you restful eye that can look upon the greatest happiness without envy.

Bless the cup that wants to overflow so that golden waters will flow from it and carry everywhere the reflection of your joy!

Look! This cup wants to be empty again, and Zarathustra wants to be a man again.

Thus began Zarathustra's going-down.

2

Zarathustra climbed down the mountain alone and no one met him. But as he entered the forest, an old man, who had left his holy hut to search for roots, suddenly stood before him. And the old man spoke thus to Zarathustra:

This wanderer is not a stranger to me: many years ago, he passed by here. He was called Zarathustra, but he has changed.

Then you carried your ashes to the mountain; now you want to carry your fire into the valley? Don't you fear the punishment meted out to the arsonist?

Yes, I recognize Zarathustra. His eyes are clear and his mouth is not foul. Doesn't he walk like a dancer?

Zarathustra has changed; Zarathustra had been a child, Zarathustra has awakened. What do you want now with the sleepers?

You lived in solitude as in the sea, and the sea carried you. Why would you want to go ashore? Why would you want to haul around your own body again?

Zarathustra answered: "I love man."

Well, why did I go into the forest and into the wilderness? asked the saint. Wasn't it because I loved man too much? Now I love God; man I do not love. For me, man is too imperfect a thing. To love man would kill me.

Zarathustra answered: "What did I say about love! I am bringing men a gift."

Don't give them anything, said the saint. It would be better if you take part of their load and help them carry it—that would do them the most good, if only it would do you good. And if you want to give them something, give them nothing more than alms, and let them beg for that!

"No," answered Zarathustra, "I won't give them any alms. I am not poor enough."

The saint laughed at Zarathustra and spoke thus: See to it that they accept your treasures. They don't trust hermits and they don't believe that we come in order to give gifts. Our steps sound too lonely through the streets. And if at night in their beds they hear a man walking by long before the sun has risen, they probably ask themselves: where is that thief going?

Don't go to man, stay in the forest! It would be better to go to the animals! Why don't you want to be as I am—a bear among bears, a bird among birds?

"And what does the saint do in the forest?" asked Zarathustra.

The saint answered: I make up songs and sing, and as I am making up songs, I laugh and I weep and I hum; thus I praise God. With singing, weeping, and humming I praise the God who is my God. What sort of gift are you bringing us anyway?

When Zarathustra heard these words, he told the saint farewell and said: "What do I have to give you! But let me go quickly, lest I take something from you!"—And so they parted from one another, the old man and the man, laughing as two boys laugh.

But when Zarathustra was alone again, he spoke thus to his heart: "Is it possible! That this old saint in his forest has not yet heard that *God is dead*!

3

When Zarathustra came into the town nearest the forest, he found that many people had gathered on the marketplace, for they had heard that a tightrope walker would be performing. And Zarathustra spoke thus to the people:

I will teach you about the superman. Man is something that should be overcome. What have you done to overcome him?

All previous creatures have created something beyond themselves: and now you want to ebb this great tide, and even go back to the animals, rather than overcome man?

What is the ape to man? A joke or a painful embarrassment. And that is just what man should be to superman: a joke or a painful embarrassment.

You have made your way from worm to man, and there is still a lot of worm in you. Once you were apes, and even now man is more of an ape than any ape. [. . .]

Let me teach you about the superman!

The superman is the meaning of the earth. Let your will say: the superman *shall be* the meaning of the earth!

I implore you, my brothers, *remain true to the earth* and do not believe those who speak to you about otherworldly hopes! They are poisoners, whether they know it or not.

Despisers of life is what they are; having poisoned themselves, they are dying. The earth has grown tired of them, so let them go!

To sin against God was once the greatest sin, but then God died, and so the sinners died as well. Now to sin against the earth is the worst thing, as is holding the entrails of the unknowable in higher esteem than the meaning of the earth!

The soul once looked down contemptuously on the body; back then this contempt was most virtuous—the body was supposed to be thin, ghastly, famished. In this way, the soul thought it could escape the body and earth itself.

But this soul itself was thin, ghastly, famished; this soul lusted after atrocities!

But you too, my brothers, tell me: what does your body say about your soul? Is not your soul poverty and filth and wretched contentment?

To tell the truth, man is a polluted stream. You would have to be the sea itself in order to take in this polluted stream without becoming unclean.

Let me teach you about the superman: he is this sea, he can take in your great contempt.

What is the greatest thing that you can experience? It is the hour of the great contempt, the hour in which you become disgusted by your happiness, and by your reason and your virtue.

The hour when you say: "What does my happiness matter! It is poverty and filth and wretched contentment. But my happiness should justify existence itself!"

The hour when you say: "What does my reason matter! Does it crave knowledge as the lion his food? It is poverty and filth and wretched contentment!"

The hour when you say: "What does my virtue matter!" It has not yet made me enraged. How tired I am of my good and my evil! All that is poverty and filth and wretched contentment!"

The hour when you say: "What does my justice matter! I do not see that I am fire and flames, and yet the just man is fire and flames!"

The hour when you say: "What does my pity matter! Isn't pity the cross on which He who loves man is nailed? But my pity is no crucifixion."

Have you ever spoken like that? Have you ever cried out like that? That I would have already heard you cry out like that!

It is not your sins that cry out to heaven, but your modesty, the very miserliness of your sins cry out to heaven.

Where is the lightning to lick you with its tongue? Where is the madness to infect you with?

Let me teach you about the superman: he is this lightning, he is this madness!

When Zarathustra had spoken thus, someone from the crowd cried out: "This tightrope walker has had a lot to say to us, now let us see what he has to show us!" The people laughed at Zarathustra. But the tightrope walker, thinking the words were meant for him, began to perform.

4

Zarathustra continued to watch the people in amazement. Then he spoke thus:

Man is a rope, tied between animal and superman — a rope over an abyss.

A dangerous crossing, a dangerous along-the-way, a dangerous glance backward, a dangerous shuddering and standing still.

What is great about man is that he is a bridge and not an end; what can be loved in man is that he is a *going-through* and a *going-under*.

I love those who do not know how to live, unless it is by going down, for those are the ones going across.

I love the great despisers, because they are the great reverers, arrows of longing shot across to the other shore.

I love those who don't first look behind the stars to find a reason to go down and to sacrifice themselves, but who sacrifice themselves for the earth so that the earth might someday belong to the superman.

I love him who lives to know and who wants to know so that the superman can live. And thus he wants to go under.

I love him who works and constructs in order to build a house for the superman and to prepare the earth, the animals, and the plants for him, for thus he wants to go under.

I love him who loves his virtue, for virtue is the will to go under and an arrow of longing.

I love him who does not hold back for himself a drop of spirit, but wants to be entirely the spirit of his virtue and thus he crosses over the bridge as spirit.

I love him who makes out his virtue, his passion, and his fate: thus for the sake of his virtue he wants to live on and to live no longer.

I love him who does not want to have too many virtues. One virtue is more virtue than two, because it is more of a knot onto which fate has strapped itself.

I love him who squanders his soul, who neither seeks nor offers thanks, because he always gives away and does not preserve himself.

I love him who is ashamed to see the dice fall in his favor and who then asks: am I then a cheat? For he wants to perish.

I love him who casts golden words before his deeds and always does more than he promised, for he wants to go under.

I love him who justifies the men of the future and redeems the men of the past, for he wants to perish on account of the men of the present.

I love him who chastises his God because he loves his God, for he must perish by the rage of his God.

I love him whose soul is deep even when it is wounded, and whom even a small experience can destroy: thus he goes gladly over the bridge.

I love him whose soul is overflowing so that he forgets himself and all things are in him: thus all things become his going-under.

I love him who has a free spirit and a free heart; thus his head is only the innards of his heart, and his heart drives him to go under.

I love all those who resemble heavy drops of rain, falling one by one out of the dark cloud that hangs over mankind: they prophesy the coming of lightning and as prophets they perish.

See, I am the prophet of lightning, a heavy drop of rain from the cloud: but this lightning is called superman.

5

As soon as Zarathustra had spoken these words, he looked at the people and fell silent. "There they stand," he said to his heart, "they laugh; they do not understand me, I am not the mouth for these ears."

Does one have to box their ears before they learn to hear with their eyes? Does one have to rattle about like kettledrums or Holy Rollers? Or will they only believe those who stammer?

They have something in which they take pride. What is it again that makes them proud? Culture is what they call it; it distinguishes them from goatherds.

That is why they do not like hearing the word "contempt" used to describe them. So let me speak to their pride.

So let me speak about the most contemptible thing: that is, *the last man*.

And thus spoke Zarathustra to the people:

The time has come for man to set himself a goal. The time has come for man to plant the seed of his greatest hope.

The soil is still rich enough, but one day it will be impoverished and tamed, and high trees will no longer be able to grow out of it.

Pay attention! The time is coming when man no longer shoots the arrow of his longing beyond man, when the string of his bow will have lost its twang!

Let me tell you: one must still have chaos in oneself in order to give birth to a dancing star. Let me tell you: you still have chaos in yourselves.

Pay attention! The time is coming when man will give birth to no more stars. Pay attention! The time of the most contemptible man is coming; that is the man who no longer will feel contempt for himself.

See! I am showing you *the last man*.

"What is love? What is creation? What is longing? What is a star?"—thus asks the last man, and he blinks.

The earth has become small and on it hops the last man who makes everything small. His race is as ineradicable as fleas; the last man lives longest.

"We have discovered happiness," say the last men and they blink.

They have left the places where the living was hard; after all, they need warmth. They still love their neighbor and rub up against him; after all, they need warmth.

To become sick or be suspicious is regarded as a sin; one walks about carefully. Only a fool still stumbles over stones or human beings!

A little poison now and then makes for pleasant dreams, and a great deal of poison a pleasant death.

They still go to work, for work is a form of entertainment. But they make sure the entertainment is not too strenuous.

They are neither rich nor poor; both are too troublesome. Who wants to rule anymore? Who wants to obey anymore? Both are too troublesome.

No herdsman and one herd! Everyone wants the same thing. Everyone is the same. Whoever feels otherwise, goes into the madhouse—voluntarily.

"Once upon a time the whole world was mad," say the most refined and they blink.

They are clever and know everything that has happened, so there is no end to their mockery. They still quarrel, but they make up quickly—otherwise they would get a stomachache.

They have their little pleasures by day and their little pleasures by night, but what they really revere is good health.

"We have discovered happiness," say the last men and they blink.

And with this Zarathustra's speech, which can be called "the prologue," ended, since at this point the shouting and yearning of the crowd interrupted him. "Zarathustra, give us your men," that is what they cried, "turn us into these last men! We'll let you have the superman!" And all the people cheered and clucked their tongues. But Zarathustra grew sad and said to his heart:

They do not understand me, I am not the mouth for these ears.

I suppose I lived too long in the mountains, listened too attentively to the brooks and the trees; now I talk to them as to goatherds.

My soul is unmoved and bright as the mountains in the morning. But they think I am cold and am a jester with terrible jokes.

And now they look at me and laugh, and laughing, they even hate me. There is ice in their laughter.

6

But then something happened that silenced every mouth and riveted every eye. For in the meantime, the tightrope walker had begun to perform: he had stepped out from a small door and was walking across the rope, which was stretched between two towers and suspended over the marketplace and all the people. Just as he reached the middle, the door opened one more time and a brightly dressed fellow looking like a buffoon jumped out and with quick steps followed after the first one. "Keep going, lamefoot," he shouted in a frightening voice, "keep going, you lazybones, you huckster, you pale face, or I'll soon be tickling you with *my* heel. What are you doing here between two towers? You belong in the tower. You should be locked up for blocking the way of a better man!" And with every word, he came closer and closer. But when he was just one step behind him, the terrible thing happened that silenced every mouth and riveted every eye. He screamed like the devil and jumped over the first fellow who was in his way. But this one then, when he saw his rival win, lost his head and the rope. He threw away his pole and plunged even faster, head over heels, into the depths. The marketplace and the people in it were like a sea in a storm; they tumbled this way and that, especially at the very place where the body would have to come crashing down.

Zarathustra, however, stood still, and it was right next to him that the body fell, horribly battered and broken, but not yet dead. After awhile, the shattered man regained consciousness and saw Zarathustra kneeling next to him. "What are you doing here?" he finally asked. "I have known for a long time that the devil would trip me up. Now, he wants to drag me to hell. Will you stop him?"

"I swear it, my friend," answered Zarathustra, "all these things that you are talking about don't exist: there is no devil and there is no hell. Your soul will be dead even before your body. Fear nothing further!"

The man looked up suspiciously. "If you are telling the truth," he said finally, "then I will have nothing to lose, if I lose my life. I am not much more than an animal who has finally been taught how to dance by being hit and starved."

"Not at all," said Zarathustra, "you have made danger your calling, there is nothing disrespectful in that. Now you will perish as a result of your calling; for that I will bury you with my own hands."

As Zarathustra said these words, the dying man fell silent. But he moved his hand, as if to take Zarathustra's in thanks.

7

In the meantime, evening arrived and darkness fell over the marketplace. The people scattered, for even curiosity and horror became tiresome. But Zarathustra remained with the dead man, and, deep in thought, he lost track of time. Eventually, it was night and a cold wind blew over the solitary man. Zarathustra got up and said to his heart:

Really, that was a fine catch of fish you brought in today, Zarathustra! Not a human being, but at least a corpse.

Human existence is eerie and still without meaning: a buffoon can prove to be fatal.

I want to teach men the meaning of their existence, which is the superman, the lightning that strikes out of the dark cloud that is man.

But I am still far away, and my meaning does not make sense to them. To men, I am still a cross between a fool and a corpse.

Dark is the night, and dark are Zarathustra's journeys. Come on, you cold and stiff companion! I will carry you to where I can bury you with my own hands.

8

As Zarathustra said this to his heart, he picked up the corpse on his back and went on his way. He had not gone a hundred steps, when a man crept up to him and whispered in his ear—and look! It was the buffoon from the tower. "Leave this town, Zarathustra," he said, "many people hate you here. You are hated by the good and the righteous, who consider you their enemy and despiser. And you are hated by the believers of the true faith, who consider you a danger to the people. You were lucky because they laughed at you, and, really, you did speak like a buffoon. You were lucky that you took care of that dead dog; when you humbled yourself in that way you saved your own life for today. But leave this town immediately—or else tomorrow I will jump over you, the living over the dead." With these words the man vanished; but Zarathustra continued on through the dark streets.

At the town gate, he encountered the grave diggers, whose torches lit up his face. They recognized Zarathustra and made fun of him: "Zarathustra is carrying off the dead dog. Isn't that nice that Zarathustra has become a grave digger! Our hands are too fine for this roast. Does Zarathustra want to steal this bite from the devil? Good luck, then, and good appetite! Just as long as the devil isn't a better thief than you, Zarathustra!—he'll steal you both, he'll devour you both!" They laughed and huddled together.

Zarathustra did not say a word and went on his way. After two hours, past woods and swamps, he had heard the hungry cry of the wolves for so long that he himself became hungry. So he stopped at a lonely house in which a light was burning.

My hunger has ambushed me, like a robber, said Zarathustra. In woods and swamps, my hunger has ambushed me, and in the dead of night.

What strange moods my hunger has. It often only comes after mealtimes, and today, it didn't come at all: where could it have been?

With that, Zarathustra knocked on the door of the house. An old man with a lantern appeared and asked: "Who is it that comes to me and to my restless sleep?"

"A living man and a dead man," said Zarathustra. "Let me eat and drink, I forgot to do so during the day. According to the wise man, he who feeds the hungry restores his own soul."

The old man disappeared, but came right back and offered Zarathustra bread and wine. "This is bad country for the hungry," he said, "that is why I live here. Both men and animals come to me, the hermit. But ask your companion to eat and drink, he is more weary than you." Zarathustra replied: "My companion is dead, I will hardly be able to persuade him to do so." "I don't care," said the old man peevishly. "Whoever knocks at my house should also accept what I have to offer. Eat and farewell!"

Thereupon Zarathustra walked two more hours, trusting the path and the light of the stars; he was used to walking at night and loved to look into the faces of everything that was asleep. When morning dawned, Zarathustra found himself deep in the woods without any sign of a path. So he placed the dead man in the hollow trunk of a tree to protect him from the wolves and laid down on the mossy ground. He quickly fell asleep, his body tired but his soul unmoved.

9

Zarathustra slept for a long time; not only did dawn pass over his face, so did the whole morning. Eventually his eyes opened. Zarathustra looked into the forest in astonishment; he looked into himself in astonishment. Then he quickly got to his feet, like a seafarer who suddenly has sighted land, and he rejoiced, for he saw a new truth. And thus he said to his heart:

It dawned on me: I need companions, living ones, not dead corpses which I carry about wherever I go.

What I need are living companions who will follow me because they want to follow themselves—wherever I go.

It dawned on me: Zarathustra should not be speaking to the people but to companions! Zarathustra should neither be the herd's man nor its dog!

To lure as many as possible from the herd—that is why I came. The people and the herd shall become angry with me; Zarathustra wants the herdsmen to think of him as a thief.

I say herdsmen, but they call themselves the good and the righteous! I say herdsmen, but they call themselves the believers of the true faith.

See the good and the righteous! Whom do they hate most of all? He who breaks the tablets of their values, the breaker, the lawbreaker— yet he is one who is the creator.

See the believers of all faiths! Whom do they hate most of all? He who breaks the tablets of their values, the breaker, the lawbreaker— yet he is one who is the creator.

The creator seeks companions, not corpses, and not the herd and not the believers. The creator seeks fellow creators who will write new values on new tablets.

The creator seeks companions, and fellow harvesters for everything around him is ripe for the harvesting. But he lacks the hundreds of sickles he needs, so he tears off the ears of corn and is angry.

The creator seeks companions, those who know how to whet their sickles. They will be regarded as destroyers and as despisers of good and evil. But they are the harvesters and the rejoicers.

Zarathustra seeks fellow creators, Zarathustra seeks fellow harvesters and fellow rejoicers: what can he do with herds and herdsmen and corpses?

And you, my very first companion, farewell! I buried you well in your hollow tree; I have hidden you well from the wolves.

The time has come to part. A new truth came to me from one dawn to another.

I shall be neither a herdsman nor a grave digger. I don't even want to talk again to the people; I have spoken for the last time to a dead man.

I want to be among the creators, the harvesters, the rejoicers. I want to show them the rainbow and all the steps up to the superman.

I will sing my song to the hermits, to the lonesome and the twosome. And whoever can hear the unheard, I want to make his heart heavy with my happiness.

I want to get to my goal, I want to go my way; I will jump over the indecisive and the dawdlers. Thus let my going be their going under!

10

This is what Zarathustra said to his heart as the sun stood at noon. He looked up questioningly at the sky and then he heard the piercing cry of a bird. And see! An eagle was making wide circles through the air, and from it was hanging a serpent, not like prey but like a friend, for it had coiled itself around the eagle's neck.

"Those are my animals!" said Zarathustra, whose heart leapt with joy.

"The proudest creature under the sun and the wisest animal under the sun—they have set out on an expedition."

"They want to discover whether Zarathustra is still alive. Am I really still alive?"

"I found it more dangerous to live among men than among animals; Zarathustra is following a dangerous road. Let my animals lead me!"

As soon as Zarathustra had said this, he recalled the words of the saint in the forest, sighed, and spoke thus to his heart:

"I want to be wiser! Wise through and through, like my serpent here!"

"But that is asking the impossible, so what I do ask is that my wisdom always be accompanied by my pride!"

"And were my wisdom to desert me—how it loves to fly away!—then let my pride fly with my foolishness!"

Thus began Zarathustra's going-under.

ON THE THREE METAMORPHOSES

I can name you three metamorphoses of the spirit: how the spirit becomes a camel; the camel, a lion; and finally the lion, a child.

There are many heavy things for the spirit, the strong spirit of burden that commands our respect: its strength longs for all that is heavy, the most heavy.

What is heavy? this is what the spirit of burden asks, how it kneels down like a camel wanting to be well loaded.

What is the heaviest thing, you heroes, that I may take it on and exult in my strength? this is what the spirit of burden asks.

Wouldn't it be this: to debase yourself in order to wound your pride? to display your foolishness in order to mock your wisdom?

Or is it this: to abandon the cause, just as it has triumphed? to climb high mountains in order to tempt the tempter?

Or is it this: to feed upon the acorns and grass of knowledge and, for the sake of truth, to starve the soul?

Or is it this: to be sick and to send away the consolers, to make friends with the deaf, who never hear what you want?

Or is it this: to wade into foul waters, if they are the waters of truth, and not be bothered by the cold frogs and hot toads?

Or is it this: to love those who despise us, and to give our hand to the ghost whenever it wants to frighten us?

The spirit of burden takes all these most heavy things on itself and, like a camel speeding its burdens across the desert, itself speeds into the desert.

In the loneliest desert the second metamorphosis takes place; here the spirit becomes a lion who wants to conquer his freedom and be master in his own desert.

Here he seeks for his final master in order to make him his enemy and his final God, in order to achieve victory over the great dragon.

Who is the great dragon whom the spirit no longer recognizes as master and God? The great dragon is called "thou shalt." But the spirit of the lion says, "I will."

"Thou shalt" lies in wait, glittering in gold, each dragon scale sparkling a golden "thou shalt!"

The values of thousands of years glimmer on these scales and thus speaks the most powerful dragon of all: "All values of all things glimmer on me."

"All values have already been created and I am these created values. There shall be no more 'I will!'" Thus speaks the dragon.

So, my brothers, what do we need the lion of the spirit for? In what way isn't the beast of burden, which renounces and reveres, good enough?

To create new values—not even the lion can do that. But the lion can create the freedom to create—that is in his power.

To create freedom for itself and to say a sacred No even to duty, that, my brothers, is what the lion is for.

To seize the right to create new values is the most terrible thing for an all-revering beast of burden. It is theft and therefore a matter for the beast of prey.

It used to love the "thou shalt" as the most sacred. Now it has to scatter the sacred to the winds and steal back freedom from his first love. The lion is needed for this theft.

But tell me, my brothers, what can the child do that the lion cannot? Why does the preying lion have to become a child?

The child is innocence, and forgetting, a new beginning, a gamble, a setting the wheel into motion, a first movement, a sacred Yes.

To play the game of creation, my brothers, you need to have this sacred Yes: the spirit now wills *its own* will, and the man who has been lost in the world now conquers *his own* world.

I have named you three metamorphoses of the spirit: how the spirit came to be a camel; the camel, a lion; and finally the lion, a child.

Thus spoke Zarathustra. [. . .]

ON THE THOUSAND AND ONE GOALS

Zarathustra saw many lands and many peoples, and so he came to discover the good and evil of many peoples. Zarathustra found no greater power on earth than good and evil.

No people could exist without first judging; but if it wanted to preserve itself, it could not judge the way its neighbor judged.

I found it to be thus: many things that one people found good, were scorned and disgraced by another. What I found to be called evil here, was decked out with the most regal honors there.

Never did one neighbor understand another. Always his soul was astonished by the madness and evil of his neighbor.

Over every people hangs a tablet of good virtues. See, it is the tablet of its overcomings; see, it is the voice of its will to power.

Praiseworthy is what it considered difficult; what seems both necessary and difficult is called good, and whatever in the time of greatest need also liberates, the most difficult and rare, it knows to be sacred.

Whatever enables a people to rule and conquer and sparkle, to the dread and envy of its neighbors, is considered, first and foremost, the measure and meaning of all things.

Truly, my brother, once you have recognized the adversity and land and sky and neighbors of a people, then you have surely understood the laws of its overcomings and the reason it climbs this particular ladder to its aspirations.

"You should always be the first, ahead of the others; your jealous soul should love no one, unless it is your friend"—these words once made the soul of a Greek tremble, with them he followed his path to greatness.

"Speak the truth and handle bow and arrow well"—these words seemed both dear and difficult for the people whose name I carry— the name that for me is both dear and difficult.

"Honor your father and mother and follow their will to the root of your soul"—another people displayed this tablet of overcoming and thereby became powerful and eternal.

"Remain faithful and, for the sake of faith, be willing to honor and sacrifice for even evil and dangerous causes"—instructed in this way, another people mastered itself and in this self-mastery became pregnant and heavy with great aspirations.

Truly, men made all their good and evil for themselves; they did not take it, they did not find it, it did not fall to them as stars from heaven.

Man first gave things value in order to preserve himself. He alone created the meaning of things, a human meaning! That is why he calls himself "Man," that is, the judger.

Judging is creating; understand that, you creators! Judging is itself the jewel of all treasures judged to be valuable.

There is value only because there is judgment, and without judgment the nut of existence would be hollow. Understand that, you creators!

Values change because their creators change; whoever is to be a creator necessarily destroys.

Creators were first people and only later individuals; indeed, the individual himself is only a very recent creation.

People used to hang a table of virtues over themselves. The love that wanted to rule and the love that wanted to obey together created such tablets.

The happiness found in the herd is older than the happiness found in oneself, and as long as good conscience corresponds to the herd, only the bad conscience can say "I."

Truly, that clever, loveless "I," which seeks its advantage by using so many others, is not the offspring of the herd but its downfall.

It was always men of love, and creators, who created good and evil. All designations of virtue glow with the fire of love and the fire of wrath.

Zarathustra saw many lands and many peoples. Zarathustra found no greater power on earth than the works of love: they are called "good" and "evil."

Truly, this power to praise and rebuke is a monster. Tell me brothers, who will subdue it for me? Tell me, who will throw a yoke over the thousand necks of this single monster?

There have been one thousand goals up to now because there have been one thousand people. But the yoke for these one thousand necks is still lacking, the one goal is still lacking.

And tell one more thing, brothers: if humanity is still lacking the goal, isn't it humanity itself that is still lacking?

Thus spoke Zarathustra.

ON THE WAY OF THE CREATOR

My brother, do you want to go into solitude? Do you want to find the way to yourself? Pause for a moment and listen to me.

"He who seeks his way, easily loses his way. To separate yourself is a crime." Thus speaks the herdsman. And you have belonged to the herd for a long time.

The voice of the herd will still reverberate inside you. When you say, "I no longer share with you a conscience," it will be a trial and an agony.

See, it is still this same shared conscience that is the cause of your agony, and the last glimmers of this conscience are still glowing in your misery.

But do you want to go the way of your misery, which is the way to yourself? Then show me that you have the right and the strength to do so!

Are you a new strength and a new right? A first movement? A setting the wheel into motion? Can you compel the stars to revolve around you?

There is so much lust for great heights! There are so many convulsions of ambition! Show me that you are neither lustful nor ambitious!

There are so many great thoughts that do nothing more than bellows: they puff and end up emptier.

You call yourself free? Then let me hear that you have ruling ideas and not just that you have escaped a yoke.

Should you have even escaped a yoke? There are those who throw away their last value when they cast off their servitude.

Free from what? What is that to Zarathustra? But your eyes should tell me clearly: free *for* what?

Can you make for yourself good and evil and can you hang your own will over yourself as a law? Can you be your own judge and the avenger of your law?

It is terrible to be alone with the judge and avenger of your own law. That is how a star is cast out into the barren void and into the icy ether of solitude.

Being alone, you are still suffering many things. Today you still have your courage intact and all your aspirations.

But the day will come when solitude will make you weary, when your pride will crumple up and your courage will break. The day will come when you will scream: "I am alone!"

The day will come when you will no longer see what makes you exalted, and you will see all too closely what makes you base. Your own raised-up figure will frighten you like a ghost. The day will come when you will scream: "Everything is false!"

There are feelings that want to kill the solitary man; if they do not succeed, well, then, they have to die themselves! But can you stand to be a murderer?

My brother, have you ever known the word "contempt"? And the anguish of your justice in being just to those who despise you?

You force many people to reconsider their views of you. They will hold that against you. You grew close to them and yet passed them by; they will never forgive you.

You pass them by, but the higher you climb, the smaller you appear to their eye of envy. But most of all they hate those who can fly.

"How can you treat me with justice?"—this is what you have to say—"I accept your injustice as my due."

They will throw dirt and injustice at the solitary man. But, my brother, if you want to be a star, you cannot shine any less brightly!

And beware of the good and the righteous! They love to crucify those who make for themselves their own virtues—they hate the solitary man.

Beware also of that sacred simplicity. Anything that is not simple is not sacred to them. They like to play with fire as well—the fire at the stake.

And beware also of the grip of your own love! The solitary man extends his hand too quickly to those he encounters.

To some men you should not extend your hand, but your paw; and I want your paw to have claws.

But the worst enemy whom you will encounter will always be yourself; you are lying in wait for yourself in hollows and woods.

Solitary man, you are going the way to yourself! This way leads past yourself and your seven devils! You will be your own heretic and witch and fortune-teller and fool and doubter and evildoer and villain.

You must be ready to set yourself on fire with your own flame; how could you become new, if you had not first become ashes?

Solitary man, you are going the way of the creator: you want to create a god for yourself out of your seven devils!

Solitary man, you are going the way of the man of love; you love yourself and for that reason you despise yourself as only a man of love can despise.

The man of love wants to create because he despises! What does he know about love who has not had to despise the very thing he loved!

My brother, go into solitude with your love and with your creation; only much later will justice catch up with you.

My brother, go into your solitude with my tears. I love those who want to create beyond themselves and perish.

Thus spoke Zarathustra.

ON THE BLESSED ISLANDS

The figs are falling from the trees; they are good and sweet. They fall, and their red skins split. I am a north wind to ripe figs.

Thus, like figs, these teachings fall to you, my friends: drink their juice and their sweet flesh! It is autumn around us and a clear sky and afternoon.

See the abundance around us! In the midst of all this bounty it is wonderful to look out on distant seas.

Once you said "God" when you looked out on distant seas, but now I have taught you to say "superman."

God is a supposition, but I do not want your supposing to reach any further than your creative will.

Could you *create* a god? Well then, don't speak to me about all the gods! But you could create the superman.

Perhaps not you yourselves, my brothers! But you could turn yourselves into the fathers and forefathers of the superman, and this would be your finest creation!

God is a supposition, but I want your supposing to be limited to what is conceivable.

Could you *conceive* a god? This would mean a will to truth that would transform everything into what could be conceived by man, what could be seen by man, what could be felt by man. You should follow your own senses to the end!

You should first create for yourselves what you have up to now called the world; the world should be created in your image, by your reason, your will, your love! It should be created for your bliss, you seekers of knowledge!

And how can you endure life without this aspiration, you seekers of knowledge? You should not make your home either in the incomprehensible or in the irrational.

But let me reveal my heart to you entirely: *if* there were gods, how could I endure not to be a god. *Thus* there are no gods.

Though this was the conclusion that I drew, now it draws me.

God is a supposition, but who could endure all the anguish of this supposition without dying? Should the creator be robbed of his faith and the eagle of his soaring in the distance?

God is an idea that makes everything straight, crooked; all that is standing still, begins to spin. How? Has time simply run out, is all that is transitory just a lie?

To think of this, the bones feel dizzy and the stomach retches. I call it the spinning sickness to suppose such a thing.

I call it evil and antihuman: all these teachings of the one, the perfect, the unmoved, the sated, and the intransitory!

All that is intransitory—that is just an image! And poets lie too much. But the best images should represent time and becoming; they should praise and justify all that is transitory!

Creation—that is the great redemption from suffering and the lightness of being. For the creator to exist there has to be suffering and much change.

Indeed, there has to be a great deal of bitter death in your life, you creators! Thus be supporters and justifiers of all that is transitory.

For the creator himself to be a child, who will be born new, he will have to want to be the woman in labor and to endure the pain of the woman in labor.

Truly, I have made my way through one thousand souls and past one hundred births and cradles. I have taken my share of leaves; I know the final heartbreaking hours.

But that is what my creative will, my destiny demands. Or, to put it more honestly: this is the destiny my will wills.

I feel hurt and imprisoned, but my will always liberates me and brings me joy.

The will liberates: that is the true doctrine of will and freedom—thus teaches you Zarathustra.

To will no more and to judge no more and to create no more! Spare me this great weariness!

When I seek and gain knowledge I feel the total delight my will takes in procreating and becoming, and if there is innocence in my knowledge then it is because it has this will to procreate.

This will lured me away from the gods and away from God; what would there be to create if the gods—actually existed!

My fervent will to create incessantly drives me toward man as the hammer is driven to stone.

You men, I see an image sleeping in the stone, it is the image of my visions! Too bad that it has to sleep in the hardest, most hideous stone!

My hammer is raging fiercely against its prison. Fragments fly off the stone: what is that to me?

I want to bring it to completion: for a shadow came to me—then it was the most quiet and the most lightweight thing. The superman's beauty came to me as a shadow. My brothers, what are the gods to me now!

Thus spoke Zarathustra.

ON REDEMPTION

As Zarathustra crossed over the great bridge one day, cripples and beggars surrounded him. A hunchback spoke to him thus:

"Look Zarathustra! Even the people are learning from you and coming to believe in your teachings. But one thing is still needed before they can believe in you completely. You will need to convince us cripples! Here you have a fine selection, so seize the opportunity! You can heal the blind and make the lame walk, and surely you can take something away from those who have too much on their backsides. In my opinion, that would be the right way to get cripples to believe in Zarathustra!"

But Zarathustra replied thus to the man who had spoken: "If you take the hump from the hunchback you take away his spirit—thus the people teach. And if you give eyes to the blind man he will see all too many horrible things on this earth so that he would curse the person who healed. And whoever makes the lame man walk does him the greatest harm, for no sooner can he walk then his vices run off with him—thus teach the people about the lame. And why shouldn't Zarathustra learn from the people, if the people learn from Zarathustra?"

"Since I have come among men, it does not matter in the least to me to see that this one is missing an eye and that one an ear and a third one a leg and there are others who have lost their tongues or their noses or their heads.

"I see and have seen worse things and many so hideous that I do not want to talk about them; some I don't even want to keep silent about. It is a matter of men who are missing everything except that they have too much of one thing, men who are nothing more than one large eye or one big mouth or one huge belly or anything else big — inverse cripples I call them.

"When I came out of my solitude and crossed over this bridge for the first time, I could not believe my eyes and looked again and again and said at last: 'That is an ear! An ear as big as a man!' I looked a little closer and saw that under the ear something else was moving, something pitifully small and miserable and gaunt. And truly, attached to this enormous ear was a small slender stalk — the stalk, however, was a man! With a magnifying glass I could even make out a tiny envious face and a puffed-up little soul dangling from the stalk. The people told me that this big ear was not only a man but a great man, a genius. But I have never believed the people when they talked about great men; I maintained my belief that it was an inverse cripple who had too little of everything and too much of one thing."

After Zarathustra had spoken thus to the hunchback and to those whose mouthpiece and speaker the hunchback was, he turned to his disciples with great displeasure and said:

"Truly, my friends, I walk among men as among the fragments and limbs of men!

"To my eyes the terrible thing is to find men shattered and scattered as if over a battlefield or a butcher's block.

"And when my eyes take flight into the past, I find the same thing: fragments and limbs and dreadful accidents — but no human beings!

"The present and the past on earth — that, my friends, is the most unendurable thing to *me*. I wouldn't know how to live if I were not also a seer of what must come.

"A seer, a willer, a creator, a future himself and a bridge to the future and, yes, even a cripple at this bridge—Zarathustra is all these things.

"You have often asked yourselves: 'What is Zarathustra to us? What shall we call him?' And like me, you answered your own questions with questions. Is he a promiser? Or a fulfiller? A conqueror? Or an inheritor? Is he the harvest? Or a ploughshare? A doctor? Or a convalescent? Is he a poet? Or a truth teller? A liberator? Or a repressor? Is he good? Or evil?

"I walk among men as among the fragments of the future, the future that I perceive. This is my art and my aim: to compose and to bring together into one everything that is a fragment and a puzzle and a dreadful accident.

"How could I endure being a man if man was not also an artist, a puzzle solver, a redeemer of accidents!

"To redeem the men of the past and to transform everything 'it was' into an 'I wanted it thus!'—that is what I would call redemption!

"Will—that is what the bringer of freedom and joy is called: thus I have taught you, my friends! And now learn this as well: the will itself is still a prisoner.

"Will liberates, but what is it that shackles even the liberator in chains?

"'It was': that is what the will's teeth gnashing and lonely melancholy is called. Powerless against what has been done, he is an angry spectator of all things past.

"The will cannot will backward. That he cannot break time and time's fancy is the will's most lonely melancholy.

"Will liberates, but how does the will propose to shake off its melancholy and mock its jailer?

"Sadly, every prisoner turns into a fool! And every imprisoned will redeems itself foolishly.

"That time does not run backward is what enrages him."

[. . .]

"Thus the will was not only liberator but also perpetrator, and he takes revenge on everything that might suffer for his inability to go back.

"This, and this alone, is what *revenge* is: the will's ill will against time and against time's 'it was.'"

[. . .]

"*The spirit of revenge*, my friends, that is the best that men have come up with so far. Wherever there was suffering, there should always be punishment."

[. . .]

"I led you from all these fables when I taught you 'the will is a creator.'

"Everything 'it was' is a fragment, a puzzle, a dreadful accident until the creative will comes up and says: 'But I willed it thus!'

"—Until the creative will comes up and says, 'But thus I will it! Thus I shall will it!'

"But did the will really speak thus? When will this happen? Has the will already been untied from its foolishness?

"Has the will redeemed itself, brought joy to itself? Has it unlearned the spirit of revenge and all teeth gnashing?

"And who taught it to be reconciled with time and something higher than any reconciliation?

"The will that is the will to power must will something higher than any reconciliation—but how will that happen? Who will teach it also to will backward?"

At this point in his lecture, Zarathustra suddenly stopped; he looked like someone scared out of his wits. With terrified eyes he looked upon his disciples. His eyes pierced their thoughts and afterthoughts. But after a little while, laughing again, he said calmly:

"It is difficult to live among men because keeping silent is so difficult, especially for the babbler."

Thus spoke Zarathustra. Meanwhile, the hunchback, his face covered, had been listening to all the talk, but when he heard Zarathustra laugh, he looked up in curiosity and slowly said:

"Why does Zarathustra speak to us differently than to his disciples?"

Zarathustra answered: "Why do you ask! Aren't you allowed to speak to a hunchback in a hunchbacked manner!"

"Well," said the hunchback, "with schoolchildren you tell tales from school.

"But why does Zarathustra speak to his children differently than to himself?"

ON OLD AND NEW TABLETS

1

Here I sit and wait, surrounded by old, broken tablets and also new half-written tablets. When will my hour come?

—the hour of going down and going under, for I want to go to men one more time.

I am now waiting for that: the signs that it is *my* hour have yet to come to me—namely, the laughing lion with the flock of doves.

In the meantime, I talk as someone who has time, for myself. No one tells me anything new, so I tell myself.

3

It was there that I also picked up the word "superman" from the path, and that man is something that must be overcome,

—that man is a bridge and not an end; counting his blessings, whether at noon or in the evening, as a way to new dawns.

—Zarathustra's word about the great noon, and whatever else I hung up over men, like the evenings' last purple afterglow.

Truly, I showed them new stars along with new nights, and over the clouds and across day and night, I spread out my laughter like a colorful canopy.

I taught them *my* art and my aim: to compose and to bring together into one everything that is a fragment and a puzzle and a dreadful accident.

—As artist, puzzle solver, and redeemer of accidents, I taught them to create the future and in creating to redeem all that *has been*.

To redeem the past of mankind and to transform every "it was" until the will says: "But I willed it thus! I shall will it thus—"

—this I called redemption—and this alone I taught them to call redemption.

Now I am waiting for *my* redemption—that I go to them one last time.

For I want to go to men one more time: I want to go under *among* them; dying, I want to give them my richest gift!

I learned that from the sun, when the superabundant star goes down: at that moment, from inexhaustible riches, it scatters gold across the sea.

—So that even the poorest fisherman rows with *golden* oars! I saw this once and did not stop weeping to see it.

Like the sun, Zarathustra wants to go down, now he sits here and waits, surrounded by old, broken tablets and also new tablets—half-written.

4

See, here is a new tablet. But where are my brothers who will carry it with me into the valley and into hearts of flesh?

My great love for the men of the distant future begs me thus: *do not spare your neighbor!* Man is something that must be overcome.

There are many paths and ways to overcoming: see to that *yourself!* But only a buffoon thinks: "Man can also be *jumped* over."

Overcome yourself even in your neighbor, and you should not let rights be given to you that you can steal for yourself!

What you do, no one can do to you. See, there is no retribution.

Whoever cannot command himself, should obey. And there are those who *can* command themselves, but much is missing before they will also obey themselves!

6

My brother, whoever is firstborn will always be sacrificed. Right now we are the firstborn.

All of us are bleeding at secret sacrificial altars, all of us are being burned and roasted in honor of old idols.

The best in us is still young; the old ones are smacking their gums. Our flesh is tender, our skin is like lambskin—of course we excite the old priests!

He still lives *inside ourselves*, the old priest who roasts our best parts for his feast. My brother, how could the firstborn not be sacrificed!

But our kind wants it thus; and I love those who do not want to preserve themselves. I love with all my love those who are going under, for they are crossing over.

7

To be truthful—only a few *are able*! And those who are able, do not want to be! Good men are the least able.

All these good men! *Good men never speak the truth!* This sort of goodness makes the spirit sick.

They give in, these good men, they give themselves up, their hearts recite, their whole being obeys: whoever obeys *does not listen to himself*!

All that the good men regard as evil must come together to form a single truth. My brothers, are you evil enough for *this* truth?

The risky adventure, the constant suspicion, the cruel No, world-weariness, the cutting into the living—how seldom do *these* come together! But these are the seeds that will create truth!

It has been *next* to a bad conscience that all *knowledge* has formed! Smash, smash for me, you seekers of knowledge, the old tablets!

8

When timbers span the water, when bridges and railings leap across the river, then, surely no one will believe the man who says, "Everything is in flux."

Even fools contradict him. "How's that?" say the fools. "Everything in flux? But there are timbers and railings *over* the river!"

"*Over* the river everything is fixed, the value of all things, the bridges, concepts, everything 'good' and 'evil'—all that is *fixed*!"

Then comes a hard winter, the breaker of rivers and animals, and even the cleverest learn mistrust. It is not only fools who then say: "Shouldn't everything—*be standing still*?"

"Fundamentally, everything stands still"—that is a fitting winter doctrine, a fine thing for a barren time, a fine consolation for hibernators and homebodies.

"Fundamentally everything stands still"—however, the thawing wind preaches to the *contrary*!

The thawing wind, a bull, a raging bull, not a plowing bull, but a destroying bull whose angry horns break the ice! And ice—*breaks bridges*!

My brothers, is not everything *in flux now*? Haven't all the bridges and railings fallen into the water? Who can still *hold on* to "good" and "evil"?

"Help us! Heal us! The thawing wind blows!"—Thus preach my brothers, in every street!

9

There is an old delusion, which is called good and evil. Up to now, this delusion has revolved around fortune-tellers and stargazers.

Once man *believed* in fortune-tellers and stargazers and *therefore* he believed: "Everything is destiny: you shall, because you must!"

Then once again man mistrusted all fortune-tellers and stargazers and *therefore* he believed: "Everything is freedom: you should, because you will!"

Up to now, my brothers, there have only been illusions, not knowledge about the stars and the future, and *therefore* there have only been illusions, not knowledge about good and evil!

10

"You shall not steal! You shall not kill!"—these phrases were once considered sacred; in their presence, people got down on their knees, bowed their heads, took off their shoes.

But let me ask you: have there ever been better thieves and murderers in the world than these sacred words?

Doesn't all life include stealing and killing? And by making these words sacred, was not *truth* itself killed?

Or was what was sacred actually a sermon of death, which contradicted and contravened all life?—Smash, smash for me, my brothers, the old tablets!

11

I pity everything in the past because I see that it has been handed over—

—handed over to the grace, the spirit, and the madness of every generation, which comes and reinterprets everything that has been as a bridge to itself!

A terrible tyrant could come, a clever fiend who with his favor and disfavor twists everything in the past into his bridge and his harbinger and herald and cockcrow.

But the other danger, which I pity as well, is this: the man of the rabble thinks back all the way to his grandfather—and with his grandfather, time stops.

Thus everything in the past has been abandoned; for it could happen one day that the rabble takes over and drowns all time in its shallow waters.

Therefore, my brothers, we need a *new nobility*, to oppose the rabble and all the tyrants and to write anew on new tablets the word "noble."

For *there to be a nobility* many noblemen are needed and noblemen of many kinds. Or as I once put it in a parable: "Godliness is many gods but no God!"

12

My brothers, I dedicate to you and direct you to a new nobility: you shall become procreators and cultivators, sowers of the future.

But not a nobility that you can buy and sell like shopkeepers with shopkeepers' gold. There is little value in anything with a price on it.

It is not where you are from, but where you are going that makes you honorable! Your will and your step—which wants to step over you—that is what makes you honorable!

Certainly not that you have served a prince—what do princes matter any more!—or that you provided a bulwark for the standing order so that it could stand more firmly!

Not that your generation became civilized at court and that you learned to stand for long hours in shallow pools, like colorful flamingos. (For courtiers are appreciated for being able to stand, and all courtiers think that part of the bliss after death is—*being able* to sit!)

Not that a spirit, which they called holy, led your forefathers into promised lands that *I* do not praise: for in the place with the worst possible trees, the Cross, grew—there is nothing to praise in this land! (And truly, on whatever crusade this "holy spirit" led its knights, goats and geese and the cross-eyed and the wrong-headed all fled *forward*!)

My brothers, your nobility shall not look backward, but *ahead*! You shall be fugitives of all fatherlands and forefatherlands!

What you shall love is your *children's land*, this love shall be your new nobility—undiscovered, in the farthest of all seas! I set your sails to search and search for it!

You shall make *amends* to your children for being the children of your fathers; *thus* you shall redeem everything in the past! This new tablet I place over you.

20

My brothers, am I really cruel? But I say: you should give a push to whatever is falling!

Everything today is falling, is decaying: who wants to preserve it! And I, I even *want* to push it!

Do you know the salacious delight which rolls stones down a steep descent?—These men of day; just see how they roll down my depths!

I am a prelude to better performers, my brothers! A precedent! *Follow* my precedent!

And if you can't teach me how to fly, then teach me—*to fall faster!*

21

I love brave men: but it is not enough to wield a broad sword—one also has to know *against whom* to wield it!

And there is often more bravery in remaining composed and passing by: *in order* to spare yourself for a worthier enemy!

You should only have enemies to hate, not enemies of whom you are contemptuous. You have to take pride in your enemy: thus I taught once before.

You should spare yourselves, my friends, for a worthier enemy: therefore, you have to pass many things by—especially the rabble that shouts in your ears all about people and nations.

Keep your eye clear of their For and Against! There is much that is right about it, and much wrong: whoever looks on just gets angry. To look in, to weigh in, all amounts to the same thing: therefore, go into the woods and put your sword to rest.

Go your *own* way! And let the people and the nations go theirs!— dark paths really, on which not a single bolt of hope flashes!

Let the shopkeepers rule where everything that still glitters—is shopkeepers' gold! The age of kings has passed: what today calls itself the people deserves no king.

See how these people all behave like shopkeepers: they take any kind of garbage to gain the slightest advantage!

They lie around in wait for each other, they lie around to wheedle something from each other—that is what they call "good neighborliness." Blessed was that distant time when a people said to itself: "I want to be—*master* over peoples!"

After all, my brothers, the best shall rule, the best also *want* to rule! And where it is taught differently, there—the best *don't exist.*

23

This is how I would have men and women: the one fit for war, the other fit for bearing children, but both fit for dancing with head and heels.

We have lost the day in which we do not dance at least once! Consider a truth false if it does not make us laugh!

25

Whoever has gained wisdom by studying ancient origins will eventually search for the springs of the future and for new origins.

My brothers, it will not be very long before *new peoples* originate and new springs will rush down new depths.

It is the earthquake—which buries many fountainheads and leaves a great deal of land parched, and which also brings hidden powers and secret things to light.

The earthquake reveals new springs. In the earthquake of ancient peoples new springs break forth.

And whoever shouts: "See, here is a well for much thirst, a heart for much longing, a will for many instruments"—around him *people* will gather who are: many experimenters.

Who can command, who must obey—*that is the experiment!* But the endless searching and guessing and failing and learning and trying again!

Human society: that is an experiment, thus I teach it. A long search: what it is looking for is a ruler!

—an experiment, my brothers, and *not* a "contract"! Smash, smash for me this word of the soft-heartedness and the half-and-half!

26

My brothers! What actually poses the greatest danger to the future of man? Is it not the good and the righteous? Is it not those who speak from their hearts and feel in their hearts: "We already know what is good and what is righteous, we already possess it; watch out for those who are still searching for it around here!"

Whatever harm the evildoers may do: the harm the good do is the most harmful of all!

My brothers, there was once a man who looked into the hearts of the good and the righteous and then said: "These are the Pharisees." But he was not understood.

The good and the righteous would not have been able to understand him: their spirits are imprisoned by their good conscience. The stupidity of the good is unfathomably clever.

But here is the truth: the good *must* be Pharisees—they have no choice!

The good *must* crucify the one who makes for himself his own virtue! That *is* the truth!

However, the next man who discovered their country—the land, heart, and soil of the good and the righteous—was the one who then said: "Whom do they hate the most?"

They hate the *creator* most, the one who smashes tablets and old values, the breaker, whom they call lawbreaker.

For the good *cannot* create; they are always the beginning of the end.

They crucify the one who writes new values on new tablets; they sacrifice the future for *themselves*; they crucify all of man's future!

The good—they were always at the beginning of the end.

27

My brothers, did you understand these words too? And what I once said about the "last man"? What poses the greatest danger to all of man's future? Is it not the good and the righteous? *Smash, smash for me the good and the righteous!*—my brothers, have you really understood these words?

28

You are running away from me? You are scared? You tremble at these words?

My brothers, when I urged you to smash the good and to smash the tablets of the good, only then did I have man embark upon his high seas.

And only now will the great fright, the great looking-around, the great sickness, the great retching, the great seasickness come.

The good taught you about deceptive shores and false securities; you were born and raised in the lies of the good. Everything has been completely distorted and falsified by the good.

But whoever discovered the land of "man," also discovered the land of "man's future." Now you shall be my seafarers, brave, patient seafarers!

Stand up straight in good time, my brothers, learn to stand up straight! The sea is stormy: many look to you to steady themselves again.

The sea is stormy; everything is at sea. Well then! Come on! You, with the hearts of old seamen!

What about the fatherland! Our sails are set far *away* to where our *children's land* lies! Way out there our great longing is raging, stormier than the sea.

29

"Why so hard!" said the charcoal to the diamond. "Aren't we close relatives?"

Why so soft? Thus *I* would ask you, my brothers, you are my brothers—aren't you?

Why so soft, so pliant and yielding? Why is there so much negation and abnegation in your hearts? Why so little destiny in your eyes?

And if you do not want to have a destiny, do not want to be pitiless, how can you come with me—and conquer?

And if your hardness will not flash and cut and cut to pieces, how can you come with me—and create?

For the creators are hard. It must be bliss to press your hands on the will of millennia as on wax—bliss to engrave the will of millennia in steel—harder than steel, more precious than steel. The most precious can only be very hard.

This new tablet, my brother, I place over you: *become hard*!

7

Beyond Good and Evil
1886

In these excerpts from Beyond Good and Evil *(1886), Nietzsche develops his ideas about the origins of morality and distinguishes between the morality of masters and the morality of slaves or of the herd, which has come to predominate in Christian Europe. He also gives us glimpses into what the "free spirits" of the future might look like as they attempt to overcome the grip of society. In the background hovers what Nietzsche considers to be the calamity of modern history, which is the revaluation of a morality of good and bad into a morality of good and evil, in which the benefits of the majority and the good of society rather than the vitality of the individual are central (section 32). One consequence of the morality of good and evil has been the one-sided divinization of nature and the*

Translated from Friedrich Nietzsche, *Jenseits von Gut und Böse*, Kritische Studienausgabe, Giorgio Colli and Mazzino Montinari, eds. (Berlin: De Gruyter, 1967ff), vol. 5.

erroneous assumption that God's laws are nature's laws (section 9), which echo themes elaborated in The Gay Science *(Document 5). But in these sections, the revaluation of morality is used as a prompt to explore morality in general. Nietzsche outlines the systems of morality that held ancient societies together and explores the values that promoted a breed of fierce, masterful men who could survive in conditions of austerity and protect the collective against enemies (sections 201, 257, and 262). It was the historic role of religion to support these masters and to offer consolation to the lower classes or to the slaves (section 61). Nietzsche repeatedly argues that not only do successful social systems require the subordination of the ruled, but great men also need the lower orders as the foundation for their own striving: Life is consistent with exploitation (sections 257, 258, and 259). However, when religion begins to tend to the suffering, to side with the weak members of society, it evolves into a slave morality characteristic of both Christianity and modern democracy (sections 61, 202, 203, and 260). But the audacious morality of the masters had always been under threat: The fearless in times of adversity need to be reined in in times of peace (section 201) and the struggles for survival create a measure of stability that fosters dissent, individuality, and, ultimately, corruption (section 262). Of course, Nietzsche's "free spirits" are highly developed individuals themselves, although they are also distinguished by their restless transformations (section 41) and sometimes by their ability to absorb different things, draw a horizon around themselves, and stand alone as unique creations (section 230). This last point connects to Nietzsche's intriguing stress on the "will to surface," which is a function of the acceptance of the self's myth about itself and is related as well to the common and average nature of social experience and language (sections 41, 43, 230, and 268). What ties the sections together is Nietzsche's contention that* "man's nature has not yet been determined" *(section 62).*

9

So you want to *live* "according to nature"? You noble Stoics,[1] how deceitful your words are! Imagine what a creature nature is, wasteful beyond measure, indifferent beyond measure, without purpose or regard, without mercy or justice, fertile and desolate and uncertain at

---

[1] *Stoics:* Members of a school of philosophy in ancient Greece that taught the need to accept the stern dictates of a rational universe.

the same time; think of indifference itself as a force—how *could* you live according to this indifference? Living—isn't that precisely wanting something other than this nature? Doesn't life consist of appraising, preferring, being unjust, being delimited, wanting to be different? And what if your imperative to "live according to nature" basically means to "live according to life"—how could you *not* do that? Why make a principle out of what you yourselves are and must be?

In truth, the matter is altogether different. You pretend to rapturously read the canon of your law in nature, but you really want the opposite, you strange actors and self-deceivers! Your pride wants to impose your ideals and your morality onto nature and make them natural. [. . .] You would like all existence to be fashioned after your own image—as an immense eternal glorification and generalization of Stoicism! For all your love of the truth, you have forced yourselves so long, so persistently, and with such hypnotic rigidity to see nature the *wrong* way, namely stoically, that you can no longer see it any differently.

32

Throughout the longest period of human history—it is called prehistory—the worth or unworthiness of an action was derived from its consequences. Neither the action itself nor its origins came into consideration. [. . .] It was the retroactive consequence of success or failure which prompted men to think of an action as good or bad. Let us call this period the *pre-moral* period of mankind: the imperative "know yourself!" was as yet unknown. However, in the last ten thousand years we have reached the point, step by step, where over large parts of the earth it is no longer the consequences, but the origin of an action which determines its worth. Taken as a whole, this is an enormous event, a considerable refinement of perspective and judgment, the unintended consequence of the dominance of aristocratic values and of the belief in "origins," the sign of a period that may be called *moral*. It is the first attempt at self-knowledge. Instead of the consequences, the origins: what a shift in perspective! Surely a transformation achieved only after protracted struggles and reversals of fortune! From then on, a fateful new superstition, a peculiar narrowness of interpretation, became dominant: the origin of an action was interpreted in the most definitive sense as origin in an *intention*. Men came to agree that the value of an action lay in the value of the intention behind it. The intention as the whole origin and prehistory of an action: across the world, almost to the present day, this prejudice has dominated moral praise, moral reproach, moral judgment, and moral philosophy. But haven't we reached the point today, thanks to the fact that men have become deeper and more self-aware, where we must once more make up our minds about this fundamental reversal and shift in values? Aren't we at the threshold of a period, which we should, in a negative sense, tentatively call *extra-moral*—today, where at least we immoralists suspect that it is precisely what is *not intentional* that determines the value of an action, and that everything about an action that is intentional, everything about it that can be seen, known, and "made conscious" is just the surface and skin of an action—skin that reveals something, but *conceals* much more? In short, we believe that intention is merely a sign and a symptom that requires interpretation, indeed a sign that means so many things that, taken by itself, means almost nothing. We believe that morality in the traditional sense, the morality of intentions, has been a prejudice, a judgment made too quickly or perhaps only provisionally, something on the order of astrology and alchemy, but something, in any case, that must be overcome. To overcome morality and, in a certain sense, even the self-overcoming of morality: this is the hard secret work which has been reserved for the finest and most honest, also for the most wicked consciences of today, as a living test of the soul.

40

Every profound spirit needs a mask; moreover, every profound spirit finds that this mask continually grows around him because he gives a consistently false, namely, *shallow* interpretation to each of his words, each of his steps, each sign of his life.

41

You must test yourself, and do so at the right time, to see whether you are destined for independence and command. You should not avoid your tests, even when they seem to be the most dangerous game you could play and even though, in the end, you are your own sole witness and judge. Do not hold onto a person, even the most dearly loved, for every person is a prison, and a hiding place. Do not hold on to a fatherland, not even when it is destitute and needs help most—at least it is easier to sever your heart from a victorious fatherland. Do not hold onto a feeling of pity, even for great men whose extreme torments and helplessness you have been allowed the chance to glimpse. Do not hold onto a science, even if it were to entice you with the most precious discoveries that seem to be reserved just for *you*. Do not hold onto your own detachment, to the voluptuous remoteness and strangeness of the bird which flees higher and higher in order to see more and more—a danger every flier faces. Do not hold onto your virtues and sacrifice your whole being to one single part of you, to your "hospitality," which is the danger of all dangers for it is the superior and rich souls who spend lavishly, almost indifferently, and make the virtue of generosity a vice. You have to know *how to conserve yourself*: the hardest test of independence.

43

Are they new friends of "truth," these up-and-coming philosophers? That is likely enough, for all philosophers have loved their truths. But they will certainly not become dogmatic. It would offend their pride as well as their taste if their truth were to become a truth for everyman, which has been precisely the secret wish and hidden meaning of all dogmas up to now. The philosophers of the future might well say: "My judgment is *my* judgment; someone else does not so easily have a right to it." It is important to get rid of the bad habit of wanting to be in agreement with many. "Good" is no longer good when your neighbor mouths it. And how can there be a "common good"! The term contradicts itself: what is common is always of little value. In the end, it must be as it is and always has been: great things are reserved for great men, the abyss for the profound, tenderness and shivers for the refined, and, in sum, all rare things for the rare.

61

The philosopher as *we* free spirits understand him, as the man with the most comprehensive responsibility whose conscience oversees the overall development of man, this philosopher will make use of religion for his project of cultivation and education, just as he will make use of existing political and economic conditions. The effort of selecting and cultivating (and this effort is always as destructive as it is creative and form giving), with which religion can help, varies according to the kind of people who stand under its spell and protection. For people who are strong and independent, who are prepared and destined to command, and who embody the reason and art of the ruling race, religion is an additional means to overcome obstacles in order to rule. It binds together the ruler with the ruled, and in doing so it betrays the ruled as it hands over their consciences to the rulers, handing over their hidden and most intimate nature, which would have preferred to elude submission. [...] Religion also gives some of the ruled the opportunity and guidance they need to prepare for eventual rule and command. These are the slowly rising orders and classes in whom, thanks to fortunate marriage customs, the strength and joy of the will, and the will to self-mastery, is constantly increasing. Religion offers them enough temptations and impulses to take the road to a higher spirituality and to experiment with feelings of great self-overcoming, of silence, and of solitude. Asceticism and Puritanism are almost indispensable instruments for educating and ennobling a race that wants to overcome its origins among the rabble and work its way up to eventual rule. And finally for ordinary people, the great majority, who exist and are only *allowed* to exist in order to serve and generally be useful, religion provides an invaluable sense of contentment with their station in life, it puts their hearts at ease, it ennobles their obedience, it gives them a little more happiness, a little more sorrow to share with one another, something to make their lives prettier and happier, to justify the routine, the meanness, the near-bestial poverty of their souls. Religion, and the meaning religion gives to life, spreads a little sunshine over these eternally tormented people and makes them bearable to themselves. Religion has the same effect as Epicurean philosophy[2] usually has on the sufferers of higher rank; it invigorates, refines, makes suffering *useful*, even restorative and justifiable. Perhaps there is nothing more honorable about Christianity and Buddhism than their ability to get even the most low-ranking to use their piety to find for themselves a place in an illusory higher order of things and thus to leave them content with the actual order, in which their lives are hard enough—and just this hardness is necessary!

62

And finally to show the negative side of these religions and to bring their extraordinary dangerousness to light: there is a high and terrible price to pay when religions do *not* serve as means for cultivation and

---

[2]*Epicurean philosophy*: A philosophical tradition in ancient Greece associated with the philosopher Epicurus, who argued for a largely mechanical conception of the universe and promoted the ethics of a quiet, but pleasurable, life.

education in the hands of philosophers, but become *sovereign* for themselves, when they want to be a final end and not a means along-side other means. As with every other species, humanity has a huge number of failures, people who are sick and infirm, people who are condemned to suffer. Outstanding examples of human beings are always the exception and, considering that *man's nature has not yet been determined*, still the rare exception. But worse still: the higher the type of man that a man represents, the greater the improbability that he will *turn out well*. Chance, the law of the absurd in the overall econ-omy of mankind, shows itself to be most destructive in its effects on higher men, whose conditions of life are demanding, subtle, and com-plicated. So how do these two great religions deal with the excess of failures? They try to care for, to keep alive whatever people can possi-bly be preserved. In fact, as religions *for sufferers*, they take the side of the failures as a matter of principle. They maintain that all those who suffer in life, as they suffer from illness, are in the right and they want to make every other feeling of life seem wrong and be regarded as unacceptable. However high you would rate this solicitous care (not least because it is also directed to the highest men, who have almost always suffered the most), in the final analysis, the *sovereign* religions bear the most responsibility for keeping the type "man" at such a low level. They preserved too much of *what should have perished*. We have to be eternally grateful to these religions, and who is so rich in grati-tude not to be impoverished at the sight of everything the "spiritual men" of Christianity have done for Europe so far! Having given com-fort to the suffering, courage to the oppressed and despairing, a leg up to the destitute, and having lured those who had become deranged and wild out of society and into the monasteries and penitentiaries of the soul, what else did they have to do in order in good conscience to preserve everything sick and suffering, that is, to tell the truth, to advance the *corruption of the European race*? Turn all values *on their head—that* is what they had to do! To crush the strong, strike down great ideas, malign the delight in beauty, to take everything auto-cratic, manly, triumphant, domineering, every instinct that belongs to the highest and most developed type of "man," and twist them into uncertainty and the agonies of conscience and self-destruction, indeed turn the whole love for worldly things and for mastery over this world into hatred of the world and worldly things. That was the task that the church set for itself and needed to set for itself until, in its view, "unworldly," "unsensual," and "higher man" were fused together into a single feeling. Suppose we could survey the fantastically painful, the crude yet exquisite comedy of European Christianity with the mocking, disinterested eye of an Epicurean god. I think there would be no end to our amazement and laughter. Doesn't it seem as if a single will has been at work in Europe for eighteen centuries in order to turn man into a *sublime monstrosity*? But if somebody approached the almost deliberate corruption and impoverishment of man as represented by European Christians (Pascal,[3] for example) with a very different intention, no longer an Epicurean, but someone with a divine hammer in his hand, he would have to cry out: "You fools, you presumptuous, pitying fools, what have you done! Was this meant for your hands! Look how you have wrecked and ruined my most beautiful stone! What presumption!" What I mean is this: Christianity has been the most disastrous form of arrogance. Men, not high or hard enough to give *human beings* artistic form; men, not strong or far-sighted enough, who lacked a superior sense of self-constraint to *let* the foundational law of a thousandfold failures and deaths prevail; men, not refined enough to see the sheer variety of ranks and differences among people—with their "equal before God," these men have ruled over the fate of Europe right up to the present day, ruled over the destiny of Europe, finally succeeding in breeding a stunted, almost ridiculous type, a herd animal, something well meaning, sickly, and mediocre, the contemporary European. . . .

199

For as long as there have been human beings, there have been human herds (families, communities, tribes, nations, states, churches) and a very large number of people who obeyed compared to the small number who commanded. In light of the fact, then, that human beings have been cultivating and practicing nothing longer and better than obedience, we can safely assume that the average person is born with an innate need to obey, which is expressed as a kind of *formal conscience* that commands: "You must absolutely do this, you must absolutely not do that," in short, "You must." This need seeks to satisfy itself and to give its form content. According to its strength, impatience, and tension, it seizes upon things with little discrimination and with raw passion, and it accepts whatever orders are shouted into its ear by parents, teachers, laws, class prejudices, and public opinion.

[3]*Pascal*: Blaise Pascal (1623–1662), a French religious thinker and mathematician who outlined and then overrode doubt about God's existence.

The strange limits to human development, the way it hesitates, is drawn out, and twists and turns, are due to the fact that the herd's instinct to obey is something best inherited and at the expense of the art of commanding. If we imagine this instinct progressing to its ultimate limits there would be no rulers or independent men at all, or they would be racked by a guilty conscience and would have to lie to themselves that they were only following orders when they were commanded. This is the state of affairs in Europe today. I call it the moral hypocrisy of the rulers. They do not know how to protect themselves from their guilty consciences other than to behave as if they were executors of more ancient or higher orders (from their ancestors, constitution, the rights, the law, or even God) or to borrow herd formulas from the herd mentality to appear as "first servant of the people" or "instruments of the common good." For his part, Europe's herd man acts as if he was the only permissible kind of man and he celebrates those attributes that make him tame, easy to get along with, and useful to the herd as the truly human virtues, namely, public spirit, goodwill, respect for others, industriousness, moderation, modesty, decency, and empathy. In those cases, where people believe they cannot do without leaders and bellweathers, they make repeated attempts to replace rulers by adding together clever herd men. This is the origin of all parliamentary assemblies, for example. What a blessing it is, for the European herd animal, what a release from an increasingly intolerable pressure, when, in spite of everything an absolute ruler does appear as was last demonstrated by the impact of the coming of Napoleon.[4] The history of the impact of Napoleon is really the history of the higher happiness this whole century attained in its most valuable men and moments.

201

As long as the utility of the herd is the only standard governing moral judgments, as long as the preservation of the community is the only thing in view, and immorality is only whatever is dangerous to the maintenance of the community, there can be no "morality of love for your neighbor." Even if there is already a small but steady show of

---

[4]*the impact of the coming of Napoleon*: Napoleon Bonaparte (1769–1821) was, in Nietzsche's view, the last great man to make an appearance in history. By making himself dictator of the French republic during the French Revolution and establishing French dominion over Europe with his armies, he proved to be a monumental historical figure.

respect for others, a little empathy, fairness, mildness, mutual aid, even if in this state of society all those drives, which will later receive the honorary designation of being "virtues," are present and ultimately constitute the concept of "morality," they do not yet belong to the realm of moral values—they are still *extramoral*. During the finest age of Rome, for example, an act that was done out of pity was considered neither good nor evil, neither moral nor immoral. And if it was praised, this praise was perfectly compatible with a kind of indignant disdain as soon as it was associated with an act that served the whole, the republica [commonwealth]. In the end, "love for your neighbor" is something conventional and willfully feigned, secondary when compared to *fear of your neighbor*. Once the structure of society appears to be established and secured against external dangers, it is this fear of your neighbor which provides new perspectives for moral judgment. Certain strong and dangerous drives such as initiative, recklessness, vengefulness, guile, rapaciousness, and ambition, which not only had to be honored for their social usefulness—under different names, to be sure, than those chosen here—but had to be nurtured and cultivated (because they were constantly needed to protect the community against its enemies), are now regarded as twice as dangerous since the channels to divert them no longer exist. Step by step, they are gradually branded as immoral and abandoned to slander. Now the opposite drives and inclinations receive moral honor; step by step, the herd instinct draws its conclusions. It is now a matter of moral perspective how much or how little danger an opinion, a situation or emotion, a will, or an aptitude poses to the community, to equality. The self-confidence of the community collapses, its faith in itself, its backbone as it were, breaks whenever the highest and strongest drives erupt in passion and carry the individual far above the average and beyond the plains of the herd conscience. Consequently, it is precisely these drives that will be branded and slandered the most. Great spiritual independence, the will to stand alone, and even great intelligence will be regarded as dangerous. From now on everything that lifts the individual above the herd and frightens neighbors is called *evil*, while a fair, modest attitude that goes along and gets along, the *mediocrity* of desires, receives the honors of morality. Eventually, under increasingly peaceful circumstances, there are fewer and fewer opportunities and less and less need to develop a sense of severity and hardness. Severity, even in matters of justice, begins to disturb the conscience. A stern and hard refinement and self-reliance are almost offensive and arouse mistrust; the "lamb," even more the "sheep," wins respect.

There comes a point in the history of society when it becomes so pathologically soft and tender that it steps in on behalf of those who harm it, *criminals*, and it does so quite seriously and honestly. To punish: that appears somehow unfair. What is certain is that the idea of "punishment" and "having to punish" is considered painful and frightening. "Isn't it enough to render him *harmless*? Why punish him as well? Punishment is terrible!" Posing this question, the morality of the herd, the morality of timidity, draws its ultimate conclusion. Imagine if danger, the grounds for fear, could be completely abolished, then this morality would be abolished as well: it would no longer be necessary, it would no longer *regard itself* as necessary! Whoever examines the conscience of present-day Europeans will find in a thousand moral recesses and hiding places the same imperative, the imperative of the timidity of the herd: "We want there to be a time when there will be *nothing* left to *fear!*" Some day—throughout Europe the will and way *to that day* is now called "progress."

202

Let's immediately repeat what we have said a hundred times, since ears nowadays are not ready for such truths—*our* truths. We know too well how offensive it sounds when someone plainly and directly classifies man as an animal; and it is almost regarded to be a *sin* when we constantly use the expressions "herd," "herd instinct," and the like to speak about the men of "modern ideas." What's the use! We can't help it because this is precisely where our new insight lies. We have found that Europe—including the countries where Europe's influence predominates—has become unanimous in its principal moral judgments. People in Europe evidently *know* what Socrates[5] thought he did not know and what that celebrated old serpent once promised to reveal—today they "know" what is good and what is evil. It is bound to sound harsh and is not easily heard when we repeatedly insist: the thing that believes it knows, that celebrates itself with its praise and reproaches and calls itself good is nothing but the instinct of the herd animal, man: the instinct which has come to the fore and come to predominate and prevail over other instincts and does so more and more in proportion to the increasing physiological standardization and

[5] *Socrates*: A fifth-century BCE Greek philosopher who, along with Plato and Aristotle, established the foundation of Western philosophy. Nietzsche admired his audacity, but condemned his idea of truth.

assimilation of which it is also the symptom. *Morality in Europe today is the morality of the herd animal*—as far as we understand the situation, this is only one variety of human morality, and the existence of other, above all, *higher* moralities beside it, in front of it, after it could and should be possible. But with all its power this one morality resists such a "possibility," such a "should." Stubbornly and unrelentingly, it declares "I am morality itself, and besides me there is no other morality!" Indeed, with the help of a religion that indulged and flattered the more sublime desires of the herd animal, it has come to the point where this morality is increasingly visible even in political and social institutions: the *democratic* movement is the heir to the Christian movement. Its advance is still much too slow and somnolent for the more impatient, for the sick and the addicts of this instinct, for we see the increasingly frantic howls, the increasingly undisguised snarling of the anarchist dogs who roam through the streets of European culture. They are purportedly opposed to the placid, industrious democrats and revolutionary ideologues, even more so to the stupid philosophasters and brotherhood fanatics[6] who call themselves socialists and seek a "free society." But actually they are united with them all in their total and instinctive hostility to every other form of society other than the *autonomous* herd (to the point of rejecting even the concepts "master" and "servant"—one of the socialist formulas is ni dieu ni maître)[7]; united with them in their tenacious opposition to every special claim or right or privilege (which ultimately means against *every* right, for if everyone is equal, no one will need "rights" anymore); united with them in their mistrust of punitive justice (as if it were an assault on the weak, an injustice against the *necessary* results of all previous societies); and likewise united with them in the religion of pity, in sympathy with whatever feels, lives, suffers (all the way down to the animals, all the way up to "God"—the extravagant notion of "pity for God" belongs in a democratic age); united with all of them in the cry and the impatience of pity, in their deadly hatred of suffering itself, in the almost feminine inability to sit by watching, to *let* someone suffer; united with them in falling involuntarily into gloom and hypersensitiv-

---

[6]*philophasters and brotherhood fanatics*: "Philophasters" is a neologism. Nietzsche is poking fun at nineteenth-century utopian philosophers, including French-born Charles Fourier (1772–1837), who envisioned phalansteries or cooperative communities to improve humankind.

[7]*Ni dieu ni maître*: Neither God nor master, a radical slogan made popular by the French socialist Auguste Blanqui when he began publishing a journal by that name in 1880.

ity, a spell which seems to threaten Europe with a new Buddhism; united with them in their faith in the morality of *shared* pity, as it if were morality itself, the height, the *attained* height of man, the only hope for the future, the solace of the present, and the great absolution from all guilt in the past; united with them in their faith in society as the *redeemer*, in short, in the herd, in "themselves." . . .

203

We have a different faith—we consider the democratic movement not only a degenerate form of political organization but a degenerate and diminished form of man, the cause of his mediocrity and devaluation. On what should *we* place our hopes?—On *new philosophers*, there is no alternative; on spirits who are strong and original enough to give impetus to opposing value judgments and to revalue and reverse "eternal values"; on forerunners, on men of the future who in the present will gather the power to force the will of millennia onto *new* paths. To teach man that the future of man is his *will*, is dependent on human will and to prepare great ventures and collective experiments in discipline and cultivation and thereby put an end to that gruesome reign of nonsense and chance called "history"—the nonsense of the "greatest number" is only its latest form. To achieve this, it will be necessary to have new kinds of philosophers and rulers, and all those obscure, horrible, well-meaning spirits that have existed on earth will pale and diminish in comparison. The images of these leaders are glimmers in *our* eyes—you free spirits, may I say this out loud? The conditions would have to be partly created, partly exploited in order to bring them into existence; the likely paths and tests that would enable a soul to grow tall and strong enough to feel *compelled* to undertake these tasks; a revaluation of values under whose new pressure and hammer a conscience would be steeled, a heart turned into steel in order to bear the weight of such responsibilities; on the other hand, the need for such leaders, the terrible danger that they might fail to come or simply turn out badly and degenerate—these are *our* real concerns and worries, you free spirits, you know that, don't you? These are the distant, heavy thoughts, the storms that cross the sky of *our* lives. There are few things as painful than to have beheld, divined, sensed how an extraordinary man lost his way and degenerated. But he who has that uncommon eye for the collective danger that "man" himself may *degenerate*, who, like us, has recognized the enormous haphazardness with which the future of man has been played—a game in which no hand, not even a "finger of God" has played along!—who has sensed the disaster that lies concealed in the idiotic ingenuousness and blind confidence of "modern ideas," and indeed in the whole Christian-European morality: he suffers from an anxiety beyond comparison. After all, with a single glance, he grasps what might yet *be made of man* with the right mobilization and intensification of forces and tasks. He knows with all the knowledge of his conscience that man has not exhausted his greatest potentialities, and he knows how often the type "man" has confronted fateful decisions and new directions. From his most painful memories, he knows even better the pathetic things that have generally brought down, broken, and themselves made pathetic those creatures rising to the highest ranks. The *total degeneration of man*, down to what socialist louts and blockheads today regard as their "man of the future"—as their ideal!—this degeneration and diminishment of man into the perfect herd animal (or, as they say, into a man in a "free society"), this animalization of men turned into stunted little animals with equal rights and equal claims is *possible*, of that there is no doubt! Whoever thinks this possibility through to the end will have one disgusting thing more than other men—and perhaps a new *task* as well.

230

The something that commands, what the people call "the spirit," wants to be master of everything that composes it and surrounds it and wants to have the feeling of being master. It wills simplicity out of multiplicity; it is a will that ties together, wrestles to the ground, seeks to dominate, truly masters. Its needs and abilities are the same ones that psychologists have identified for anything that lives, grows, and multiplies. The power of the spirit to appropriate for itself what is foreign can be seen in its strong inclination to assimilate the new to the old, to simplify diversity, to disregard or push aside total inconsistencies. At the same time, it takes certain features and lines of what is foreign, any piece of the "external world" really, and arbitrarily underscores, emphasizes, or falsifies them after its own fashion. Its intention in all this is to incorporate new "experiences," to arrange new things in old patterns—it is to grow, or, more precisely, to have the *feeling* of growth, to have the feeling of increased strength. What seems to be an opposite drive also serves this same will: a sudden resolution to remain ignorant, to remain deliberately cut off, to shut the windows, an internal No to this or that, a come-no-closer, a kind of defensive guard against many knowable things, a contentment with darkness, with a delimiting horizon, a Yes to ignorance, an acceptance of ignorance. Just how necessary all this is depends on its ability to assimilate, on its "powers of digestion," to speak metaphorically—"the spirit" really resembles a stomach more than anything else. The spirit's occasional will to let itself be deceived belongs here too, perhaps along with a sneaking suspicion that such and such is *not* the case although it will be allowed to pass anyway, with a zest for anything uncertain or ambiguous, a cheerful delight in the sheer narrowness and secrecy of a nook, in what is all too near, in the foreground, in all the things that have been enlarged, reduced, sidelined, prettied-up, a delight in the arbitrary nature of all these expressions of power. Finally, we need to add the spirit's not unproblematic readiness to deceive other spirits and dissimulate in front of them, the continual pressing and pushing force of a creative, form-giving, transformative power. In this respect, the spirit enjoys the variety and cunning of its masquerade, and enjoys as well the feeling of security it provides; after all, it is through its protean abilities that it is best protected and concealed! *This* will to appearances, to simplification, to masks, to cloaks, in short, to surface—for every surface is a cloak—is *countered* by the seekers of knowledge whose sublime inclination it is to take and *always* to take a deep, many-sided, and thorough view of things. This reveals the bloodthirstiness of intellectual conscience and taste, which every honest thinker will recognize in himself, provided he has looked at himself long and hard and is accustomed to harsh discipline and harsh words. Then he will say, "There is something bloodthirsty about the direction of my spirit"—just let the virtuous and the kindhearted talk him out of that! In fact, it would sound more polite if we would be remembered and praised not for our bloodthirstiness, but for our "extravagant honesty," we very, *very* free spirits. Maybe one day that is what we will be known for, but that day is a long way off. In the meantime, we should at least avoid tarting ourselves up with the trinkets and tinsel of morality. Everything we have done so far has made us sick of these fashions and their cheerful opulence. They are shiny, glittering, jingling, festive words: honesty, love of truth, love of wisdom, self-sacrifice for the sake of knowledge, the heroism of the truthful—these are words that make you proud. But hermits and groundhogs that we are, we have long ago convinced ourselves that all this estimable, pompous vocabulary belongs right alongside the old costumes, treasures, and gold dust of an unconscious human vanity and that beneath such flattering colors and made-up faces we will be able to make out the terrifying, underlying text of *homo natura*.[8] To translate man back into nature; to master all the vain and fanciful meanings and connotations that have been scribbled and painted over the eternal text of *homo natura*; to make sure that man from now on stands before man in the way that man today, hardened by the discipline of science, stands before the *rest* of nature, with unflinching Oedipus eyes and sealed-up Odysseus ears,[9] deaf to the songs of old metaphysical sirens who for too long have been whistling at him: "You are more! you are better! you have been made differently!"—this may be a strange and mad undertaking, but it is a *task*—who would deny that! Or put a different way: "Why knowledge at all?" Everyone will ask us about that. And when pressed, we, who have asked ourselves the same question a hundred times, we have found and can find no better answer.

257

Up to now, every enhancement of the type "man" has been the achievement of aristocratic society—and that is how it will remain—a society that believes in a long ladder of hierarchy and in the differences in the value of men and that requires slavery in some form. Without the *pathos of distance* which emerges from the ingrained differences between classes, from the way the ruling caste continuously looks out over and down upon subjects and instruments, and from the way it just as continuously obeys and commands and holds down and holds at a distance, that other, even more mysterious pathos could not have emerged: the longing for ever new widening of distances within the soul itself, the formation of ever higher, rarer, more remote, far-reaching, and comprehensive conditions, in short the enhancement of the type "man," the continual "self-overcoming of man," to use a moral formula in a supramoral sense. To be sure, there should be no humanitarian illusions about the origins of aristocratic society (which is the precondition for the enhancement of the type "man"): the truth is

[8]*homo natura*: natural man.
[9]*Oedipus eyes . . . Odysseus ears*: In ancient Greek mythology, Oedipus was the king of Thebes who unknowingly killed his father and married his mother; upon discovering that he had done so, he put out his own eyes and left the kingdom a broken man. Odysseus, a prince returning home from the Trojan War on an epic journey that is the centerpiece of Homer's *Odyssey*, knows he cannot be tempted by the Sirens he must pass but wants to hear their song, so while he has his men stop up their ears with wax, Odysseus orders them to lash him to the mast and ignore his pleading while they row to safety.

hard. Let us be blunt about the *beginnings* of every higher culture to appear on this earth! Men whose nature was still natural, barbarians in every dreadful sense of the word, predators still possessing an unbroken strength of will and desire for power threw themselves on weaker, more law-abiding, peaceful people, perhaps traders or cattle herders, or else older, worn-out cultures whose last vitality was flickering out in brilliant fireworks displays of intellect and corruption. The caste of refinement always started out as a caste of barbarianism; its superiority rested on psychological, not physical, power. It comprised the *more complete* men (which in every respect means the same thing as "the more complete beasts").

258

Corruption, as the indication that the instincts are threatened with anarchy and the foundation of emotions which is called "life" is undermined: corruption is completely different depending on the forms of life in which it appears. When, for example, an aristocracy like that of France at the beginning of the Revolution throws away its privileges with profound disgust and sacrifices itself to an extravagance of moral feeling, that is corruption.[10] This was really just the last act of a centuries-long corruption in which the aristocracy steadily relinquished its manorial powers and reduced itself to a *function* of the monarchy (and finally to its ornament and showpiece). But the essential thing in a good and healthy aristocracy is that it does *not* consider itself a function, whether of a monarchy or a commonwealth, but rather as their *meaning* and primary justification and that it accepts with good conscience the sacrifice of any number of people who for *its sake* have to be suppressed and reduced to incomplete beings, to slaves, to instruments. Its fundamental belief must be that society does *not* exist for the sake of society but only as a foundation and framework in which a carefully selected type of being is able to accomplish its higher task and raise itself more generally to a higher state of *being*: like those sun-seeking vines in Java—they are called *Sipo Matador*—which clasp themselves around the oak tree as long and as often as they

---

[10] *France at the beginning of the Revolution*: One month into the French Revolution, on the night of August 4, 1789, the representatives of the French nobility, meeting in the National Assembly, renounced their feudal privileges in anticipation of a regime in which everyone would be equal before the law. Nietzsche is appalled by this demonstration of equality.

must until finally, high above the tree, but supported by it, they are able to unfold their crowns and display their happiness in the open air.

259

To mutually refrain from injury, violence, and exploitation, to place your will alongside another's, is something that can evolve, in a certain rough sense, into good manners among individuals if the appropriate conditions are present (namely, if they are genuinely similar in strength and judgment and belong to a single group). But as soon as this principle is extended further and even becomes the *fundamental principle of society*, then it is immediately seen for what it is, that is, as a will to *deny* life, as the principle of dissolution and decay. We have to think this matter through and resist any sentimental weakness. Life itself is *essentially* appropriation, violation, the conquest of strangers and weaklings, suppression, hardness, the imposition of our own designs, assimilation, and, at the very least, at the most mild, exploitation. (What is the point of always using words that have been stamped with a slanderous intention since time immemorial?) Even that group, in which, as mentioned, individuals treat one another as equals (the case in every healthy aristocracy), must, if it is living and not dying, do everything against other groups that the individuals inside it refrain from doing to each other. It will have to incorporate the will to power, it will want to grow, cast about, pull in toward itself, and gain ascendancy, not out of any morality or immorality but because it is *alive*, and because life *is* just this will to power. Nonetheless, on no point is the overall conscience of Europeans more resistant to instruction than here; even under the guise of science, people everywhere run on about the coming conditions of society in which "the exploitative character" will disappear. To my ears that sounds like promising to invent a being without any organic functions. "Exploitation" does not characterize a corrupt or undeveloped and primitive society; it characterizes the very *essence* of being alive. It is a basic organic function, a result of the intrinsic will to power which is nothing less than the will to life. In theory this is something new, in reality it is the *primal fact* of all history; let us be at least that honest with ourselves!

260

In my wanderings through all the refined and crude moralities that have up to now appeared on earth, I found certain traits regularly reappearing together and combining until I made out two basic types and a one single basic distinction. There is a *master morality* and a *slave morality.* [...] Moral judgments have arisen either among a group of rulers which understood perfectly well its difference from the ruled, or among the ruled themselves, the slaves and dependents at every rank. In the first case, when the rulers determine what is "good," it is the exalted, proud states of the soul that are perceived as distinctive and indicative of rank. The refined man casts off those natures in which the opposite of those exalted, proud states find expression: he despises them. It should be noted immediately that the opposition "good" and "bad" means as much in this morality as "refined" and "contemptible"—the opposition "good" and "evil" origi- nates elsewhere. Despised are those who are cowardly, fearful, petty, and think narrowly in terms of utility, as are mistrustful people with their constricted perceptions, the groveler, that dog type who lets him- self be mistreated, the fawning flatterers, and, above all, liars—it is an article of faith among aristocrats that the common people are liars. "We truth tellers" is what the nobility in ancient Greece called itself. It is obvious that designations of morality everywhere applied first to *human beings* and only later, derivately, to *actions.* That is why it is a great mistake for historians of morality to start with questions such as "why are acts of compassion praised?" The refined type of man feels that *he* determines value; he does not require anyone's approval; he judges "what harms me is harmful in itself"; he knows that it is him- self that makes things honorable in the first place; he *creates values.* He honors everything that he recognizes in himself. This is a morality that glorifies the self. In the foreground, there is a feeling of abun- dance, of power that is overflowing, the happiness of the high state of tension, the consciousness of wealth that wants to give gifts and give way. The refined man also helps the unfortunate, although he never or almost never does so out of pity, but rather out of an urge generated by the excess of power. The refined man honors the man of power in himself but also the man who has power over himself, who knows when to speak and when to remain silent, who delights in being severe and hard with himself and reveres all that is severe and hard. An old Scandinavian saga puts it this way: "Wotan places a hard heart in my breast"—a fitting expression from the soul of a proud Viking. This sort of man actually takes pride in *not* being made for pity. That is why the hero of the saga adds as a warning: "if your heart is not hard when you are young, it will never be hard." Refined and brave men who think this way are at the farthest remove from the morality that regards pity or acting for others or impartiality [*désintéressement*] as the very expression of moral behavior. Belief in yourself, pride in yourself, a fundamental hostility to and irony for "selflessness" surely belong as much to a refined morality as a slight disdain for and wariness around sympathetic feelings and "warm hearts." It is the powerful who *know* how to honor, that is their art, the realm of creativity. A profound respect for age and tradition—all law rests on this twofold respect—and faith in and a predisposition in favor of ancestors and against descendants is characteristic of the morality of the powerful. By contrast, when people with "modern ideas" almost instinctively believe in "progress" and "the future" and show less and less respect for age, they betray the unrefined origins of these "ideas." Most of all, the morality of rulers is at odds with contemporary tastes by being scrupulous in the rigor of its basic principle that we are responsible only to our own kind and that we should act toward inferior beings, or anything foreign, as we please or "as the heart desires," in any case "beyond good and evil"—this is where pity and the like might have a place. The capacity and duty to remain ever grateful and ever vengeful (though only to one's own kind), subtlety when retaliating, a refined conception of friendship, a certain necessity to maintain enemies (which acts as a release for envy, aggressiveness, and arrogance—in order to be a good *friend*)—these are the typical characteristics of a refined morality which, as previously indicated, is not the morality of "modern ideas" and is therefore hard today to get a feel for, to dig out and to expose.

It is quite different with the second kind of morality, the slave morality. Assuming that the people who are abused, oppressed, suffering, unfree, unsure of themselves, and exhausted do moralize, what then would their moral judgments have in common? Most likely we would find that a suspicious pessimism about the whole condition of humanity would emerge, perhaps a blanket condemnation of humanity and its condition. The slave regards the virtues of the powerful with resentment; he is skeptical and mistrustful, he has a *well-developed* suspicion against all the "good things" that they honor. He would like to persuade himself that they are not really happy. Conversely, qualities that seek to alleviate the lot of the suffering are pulled out and cast into the light. What we would see honored here are empathy, the ready helping hand, the warm heart, patience, industriousness, humility, and friendliness. These are the most useful qualities and practically the only means to withstand the pressure of existence. Slave morality is essentially a morality of utility. Here is the point of origin of the famous opposition "good" and "*evil.*" Evil is perceived as something powerful and dangerous; it is terrible, subtle, strong, and therefore not contemptible. In a slave morality, then, "evil" inspires fear, whereas in a master morality it is "good" which inspires and intends to inspire fear, while the "bad" man is regarded as contemptible. The difference comes to a head when, following the logic of slave morality, there is a little bit of disdain, however slight and well-meaning, associated with the idea of "good," because according to the slave a person who is good is also *harmless*; he is good-natured, easy to deceive, a bit stupid perhaps, *un bonhomme.*[11] Wherever slave morality prevails, language tends to bring together the words "good" and "stupid."

One last fundamental difference: the longing for *freedom*, a feeling for happiness and for the subtleties of freedom characterizes slave morals and slave morality as surely as the capacity and enthusiasm for reverence, for devotion characterizes an aristocratic way of thinking and judging. This makes it clear why love as a *passion* (which is our European specialty) simply must be of noble origin. It is well-known that love was one of the discoveries of the poet-knights of Provence,[12] those magnificent, inventive men of the "gai saber," to whom Europe owes so much, indeed practically owes itself.

262

A *kind* of people emerges, a type grows sturdy and strong in the long struggle with essentially unchanging *unfavorable* conditions. Conversely, we know from the experience of breeders that creatures who are provided with overly rich nourishment and generally too much protection and care show the strongest tendency to variations of type and display all sorts of marvels and monstrosities (including monstrous vices). Now take an aristocratic society, the old Greek polis or Venice,[13] for example, as an organization that has been established, voluntarily or involuntarily, for *breeding*. Thrown together, the people depend on each other in order to prevail, usually because they *must* prevail or run the terrible risk of being eradicated. Here, there is none of the grace, the excess, the protection that promotes variations. This

[11] *un bonhomme*: A good guy.

[12] *the poet-knights of Provence*: In the Middle Ages, the French region of Provence, on the Mediterranean Sea, was known for its troubadour poetry and political independence.

[13] *Greek polis or Venice*: Nietzsche admired the rule of patricians both in the ancient Greek polis or city-state and in late medieval Venice.

people needs itself as a people, as something that by virtue of its hardness, uniformity, and simplicity can prevail and make itself unassailable in the permanent struggle with its neighbors or its own rebellious, hostile underclass. Long experience has shown to which qualities it owes the fact that, all gods and all men notwithstanding, it is still there, that it still continues to triumph. It calls these qualities virtues and it is these virtues alone that it cultivates. It does so severely; indeed, it seeks out severity. Every aristocratic morality is intolerant in the education of youth, in dealing with women, in marriage customs, in the relations between young and old, in penal laws (which only concern deviants). Intolerance itself is a virtue under the name "justice." In this way, a kind of people with few but very powerful characteristics, a type of stern, warlike, prudently silent men, closed-mouthed and close together (and as such with the finest feeling for the charm and nuance of society) establishes itself over the generations. As I have said, the constant struggle with unchangingly *unfavorable* conditions is the reason why this type grows sturdy and hardy. But eventually more fortunate conditions appear, the tremendous tension eases. Perhaps neighbors are no longer enemies, and there are more than enough means to secure life and even to enjoy life. In a single stroke, the bond and restraint of the old discipline breaks; it no longer seems necessary. If it were to continue it would only be as a kind of *indulgence* or antiquated *taste*. Whether as a deviation (into something higher, rarer, more refined) or as degeneration and monstrosity, variation suddenly appears in the greatest abundance and splendor. The individual dares to be individual and different. What emerges at these turning points of history are a series of magnificent, diverse, often tangled jungle-like germinations; there is a *tropical* tempo in the urgency to grow, but also astonishing destruction and self-destruction as the wildly struggling, exploding individual egos wrestle with each another "for sun and light" no longer respecting any of the limits, the restraints, or the preserves of the old morality. This was the morality that had accumulated such extraordinary strength and tightened the tension so dangerously—and now it has become "superfluous." The dangerous and eerie point has been reached when a grander, more diverse, more comprehensive life *lives itself beyond* the old morality. The "individual" appears, resolved to give himself his own laws and find the necessary arts and tricks for his own self-preservation, self-enhancement, self-redemption. There are all kinds of new what-fors and how-tos, no longer any common formulas; misunderstanding combines with disrespect; decay, corruption, and the highest desires are horribly entwined; the genius of the people overflowing from every wellspring of good and bad; the ominous simultaneity of spring and autumn, full of the new attractions and distractions that characterize corruption that is still young, energetic, and unwearied. Danger, the mother of all morality, has returned, a great danger, but this time posed by the individual, by neighbors and friends, by the street, by our own children, our own heart, in the most personal and secret places of desire and will: what will the moral philosophers of this age have to preach now? These sharp observers and loiterers discover that everything is coming quickly to an end, that everything around them decays and corrupts, that nothing will remain the day after tomorrow with one exception, one type of man, the hopelessly *mediocre*. Only the mediocre have a chance to continue on and propagate themselves. They are the men of the future, the sole survivors. "Be like them! become mediocre!" is the only morality that makes any sense any more, that will get a hearing. But this morality of mediocrity is difficult to preach!—for it can never admit what it is and what it wants! It must speak about moderation and dignity and duty and love for your neighbor—it will have a hard time *concealing its irony!*

268

What ultimately is common?

Words are vocalizations for concepts, and concepts are nothing more than particular images for a series of recurring sensations, for groups of sensations. For us to understand each other, it is not enough to use the same words; we have to use the same words for the same kinds of inner experiences; in the end our experiences must be held in *common*. That is why the people of one nation can understand each other better than people from various nations, even when they all speak the same language. Or, when people have lived together for a long time under the same conditions (of climate, soil, danger, needs, work), something *emerges*, a people who "understand each other." In every soul, the same number of often recurring experiences has prevailed over experiences that come more rarely, and thereby people come to understand each other more and more quickly. The history of language is the history of this process of abbreviation. On the basis of reaching a quick understanding, people combine with each other, more and more closely. And the bigger the danger, the greater the need to reach an agreement quickly and easily over what needs to be done. Not to misunderstand each other in a moment of danger is something human beings cannot do without in their relations with one another. In every friendship or love affair, we continue to take this test. Nothing will last if it becomes clear that one of the two uses the same words to express different feelings, thoughts, intuitions, wishes, or fears. [...] Now, assuming that adversity has brought a group of people closer together who with similar signs express similar needs and similar experiences, it would follow that the easy *communicability* of need, which in the last analysis means the experience of merely average and *common* experiences, would have to have been one of the powerful forces directing human life. People who are more similar and ordinary have and always have had the advantage; those who are more select, more refined, and more unique, or are more difficult to understand, tend to remain alone, and, in their isolation, are prone to accidents and seldom propagate themselves. Immense counterforces have to be mobilized in order to resist this natural, all-too-natural unceasing process of making man similar, ordinary, average, herd-like—*common!*

8

On the Genealogy of Morals
1887

Nietzsche described On the Genealogy of Morals, *published in 1887, as a "sequel" and "supplement" to* Beyond Good and Evil, *which had appeared a year earlier, and it is a more tightly argued, less flamboyant reconsideration of the historical and linguistic origins of the designations good and bad and the subsequent revaluation of the morality of good and bad into the morality of good and evil. In these excerpts, Nietzsche provides a more detailed historical explanation rooted in Jewish resistance to the Roman Empire and the broader Christian adoption of Jewish morality that followed. There is an edge to Nietzsche's writing on Jews, which readers today will find striking, but Nietzsche justified the Jewish*

Translated from Friedrich Nietzsche, *Zur Genealogie der Moral*, Kritische Studienausgabe, Giorgio Colli and Mazzino Montinari, eds. (Berlin: De Gruyter, 1967ff), vol. 5.

revaluation of morals whereas he had nothing but scorn for its Christian version, except in one very important respect (First Essay, sections 7–8). The revaluation of morality created depth to human beings by giving them a soul, which made them interesting and available for new experiments (First Essay, section 6, and Second Essay, section 16). In any case, even willing nothingness, as Nietzsche accuses modern people of doing, is a sign of life (Third Essay, section 28). Whereas in The Gay Science *Nietzsche scorned the lucky throws of the dice as exceptional and not telling (see Document 5, section 109), here he is delighted that men are the creatures of the games of chance. He goes on to explore both the older morality of good and bad and the distance the higher orders kept from the lower orders (First Essay, sections 2 and 4), the struggle of the powerless and the Jews against the morality of good and bad (First Essay, sections 7–9), and the attributes of the virtuous and righteous (First Essay, section 10). If what is good in the morality of good and evil speaks in the name of the powerless, has profound contempt for the powerful, and is often characterized by cleverness, which for Nietzsche is not a particularly positive attribute, then what had been good in the morality of good and bad is, Nietzsche concedes, cruel and rightfully regarded as barbaric (First Essay, sections 10, 11, and 13). Nietzsche also introduces readers to two captivating spectacles: that of the cruel, strong men in the ancient world who provided endless entertainment to the gods and that of the cruel, strong men in the Christian era, tempted by sin and tortured by bad conscience (Second Essay, sections 7 and 16). Here as elsewhere, Nietzsche loves paradoxes, the ability of the powerless, for example, to overcome the powerful with a morality of good and evil, which also turned hatred of the powerful into love for the powerless (First Essay, section 7).*

FIRST ESSAY: "GOOD AND EVIL," "GOOD AND BAD"

2

"Originally"—so [these historians of morality] decree—"unegotistical actions were praised and called good from the point of view of their beneficiaries, that is, for whom they were *useful*; over time, the reason for the praise was *forgotten* and unegotistical actions were simply regarded as good because they had been always *routinely* praised as good—as if there was something good in themselves." We can see at

once that this first proposition already contains all the typical characteristics of the idiosyncratic English psychologists—we have "utility,"
"forgetting," "habit," and finally "error." These are taken to be the
basis of the esteem in which up to now the higher type of man had
taken pride as a kind of prerogative of man as such. Now this pride *is
to be* humbled, this esteem devalued. Has this been achieved? . . . Now
it seems plain to me that this theory seeks the origin of the concept
"good" in the wrong place. It was *not* the beneficiaries of a "good"
action who came up with the judgment "good"! Instead, it was the "the
good" themselves, the refined, the powerful, the well-born, and the
high-minded who regarded and established themselves and their
actions as good, that is, first-rate in contrast to everything low, vulgar,
common, or plebian. It was this *pathos of distance* that first authorized
them to take the right to create values and to designate values. This
had nothing to do with utility. The perspective of utility is completely
out of place and inappropriate in view of the proliferation of the highest rank-ordering, rank-defying values. This sort of feeling is the opposite of the low-temperature state appropriate for a purely calculating
intelligence or a merely utilitarian calculus—not just once, for one
exceptional moment, but forever. The pathos of refinement and distance, as I said, the persistent, forceful elementary feeling of a higher
ruling order in contrast to a lower order, to those "below"—*that* is the
origin of the opposition "good" and "bad." (The right of rulers to designate names went so far that we can conceive of the origin of language
as an expression of power on the part of the rulers: they say "this *is*
thus and such," they seal everything and every event with words and
thereby take possession of them.) It is because of this origin that the
word "good" is *not* at all necessarily connected to "unegoistical" actions from the outset, as the superstitions of the genealogists of morality would have it. Only with the *decline* of aristocratic judgments of
value does the whole opposition "egotistical" and "unegotistical" impose
itself more and more on human conscience. Thus, to use my words,
the instinct of the herd finally gets its word in (and makes *words*).

4

I found myself pointed in the *right* direction by the question as to the
real etymological meanings of the term "good" as used in various languages. I found that they all revealed the *same conceptual transformation* in which everywhere "well-born" or "noble" (in the context of a
society of orders) is the basic concept from which "good" (in the context of "spiritually refined"), "noble," "spiritually developed," or a "priv-

ileged soul" developed. This transformation always ran parallel to that other one in which "common," "plebian," and "low" take on the meaning of "bad." The most convincing for the latter is the German word "schlecht" [bad] itself, which is identical with "schlicht" [plain, simple] — take "schlechtweg" [plainly], "schlechterdings" [simply] — and originally referred to the simple, common man without a derogatory implication, but simply in contrast to the refined. [. . .] This seems to be a *fundamental* insight with regard to the genealogy of morals.

6

There is a variation to the rule that the concept of political superiority always corresponds to a concept of spiritual superiority when the highest class is also a *religious* class and as a result describes itself with attributes that refer to its priestly functions. In this case, "pure" and "impure" appear for the first time as expressions of status and later evolve into a "good" and a "bad" which no longer refer to a society of orders. [. . .] The "pure" man is from the beginning a man who keeps himself clean, who abstains from certain foods said to produce skin ailments, who does not sleep with dirty women from the lower classes, who has an aversion to blood — not much more than that! Yet it is clear from the whole nature of an essentially religious aristocracy why early on precisely the opposition in values was internalized and intensified in such extreme fashion. And indeed it finally tore a chasm between man and man. [. . .] From the very beginning, there is something *unhealthy* in these religious aristocracies and in their ruling ideas which turn them away from action and alternate between brooding and emotional outbursts. [. . .] Priests make *everything* more dangerous, not only cures and remedies but also arrogance, revenge, ingenuity, extravagance, love, mastery, virtue, sickness — though it is only fair to add that on the basis of this *essentially dangerous* form of religious life that man came to be *an interesting animal* at all and that in an abstract sense the human soul gained *depth* and became *evil* — and these are exactly the two principal ways in which man is superior to the other beasts!

7

You will already have figured out how easily the religious mode of judging splits off from the knightly-aristocratic and then develops into its opposite. [. . .] The knightly-aristocratic value judgments presuppose a powerful physicality, a flourishing, abundant even overflowing health, together with everything necessary to preserve it: war, adventure, hunting, dancing, jousting, and all that promotes vigorous, free, joyful action. The refined religious value judgments have, as we have seen, other requirements: not the right things when it comes to war. As we know, priests are the *most evil enemies* to have—but why is this the case? Because they are the most powerless. Their powerlessness induces a hatred that expands into monstrous and sinister proportions, into the most spiritual and poisonous kind of hate. The great haters in world history have always been priests. No other kind of intellect can match the spirit of priestly revenge. Human history would be altogether too stupid a thing without the spirit that the powerless have introduced into it. Let us take the most important example. Everything that has been done on earth against "the refined," "the powerful," "the masters," "the rulers" is nothing to speak of in comparison to what *the Jews* have done to them. The Jews, that priestly people, who in opposing their enemies and conquerors were satisfied with nothing less than a radical revaluation of their enemies' values, that is to say an act of the *most spiritual revenge.* This was only fitting for a priestly people in whom the priestly lust for revenge was a subtle thing to see. It was the Jews who with awe-inspiring consistency dared to invert the aristocratic equation of values (good = refined = powerful = beautiful = happy = loved by God) and with the teeth of the most abysmal hatred (the hatred of powerlessness) held forth that "the wretched alone are the good; the poor, the powerless, the downtrodden alone are the good; the suffering, the needy, the sick, the ugly alone are pious, alone are blessed by God, blessedness is for them alone, and that you, by contrast, you, the refined and powerful, you are, for all eternity, the evil, the cruel, the lustful, the insatiable, the godless, you will forever be cursed and damned." . . . We know *who* inherited this Jewish revaluation . . . with the Jews *the slave revolt in morality* begins, a revolt which has two thousand years of history behind it and which has only disappeared from view because it— has been victorious.

8

You don't understand this? You don't have an eye for something that took two thousand years to achieve victory? . . . There is no reason to be surprised: all *drawn-out* things are hard to see, to oversee. *This,* however, is what happened: out of the trunk of that tree of vengefulness and hatred, Jewish hatred, out of the most deep and sublime ideal-creating, value-recreating hatred that has ever been seen on earth there grew something just as incomparable: a *new love*, the deepest and most sublime kind of love—and from what other trunk could it have grown?

9

Let's stick to the facts. The people have won—or rather "the slaves" or "the mob" or "herd" or whatever you want to call them—and if this happened because of the Jews, so be it! No people has ever had a greater world-historical mission. "The masters" have been removed; the morality of the common man has triumphed. You can also take this victory as a blood poisoning (it has mixed up the races)—I do not deny it. But there is no doubt that this intoxication has *succeeded*. The "redemption" of human beings (namely, from "the masters") is well on its way. Everything is becoming Judaized or Christianized or plebianized (what do the words matter?).

10

The slave revolt in morality begins when *resentment* itself becomes creative and gives form to values: the resentment of those creatures who have been denied the proper response of action and now find compensation in imaginary revenge. Whereas all refined morality develops expansively with a triumphant Yes to itself, slave morality on principle says No to any "as well as," to anything "different," to anything "not itself," and *this* No is its creative deed. This inversion of the eye that judges value—this *need* to direct attention to the outside rather than back to oneself—is the essence of resentment. In order to establish itself, slave morality needs a hostile outside world; in psychological terms, it needs external stimuli in order to act at all. Its action is basically a reaction. The opposite is the case with the refined value judgment: it acts and grows spontaneously, it seeks its opposite in order to affirm itself in renewed appreciation and delight. Its negative outlook—"low," "common," "bad"—is a pale secondary contrast to its positive outlook. Filled through and through with life and passion . . . the refined value judgment might well misunderstand the sphere it despises, which is the sphere of the common man, the lower class, but it has to be noted that in any case the feeling of contempt, of looking down upon, of overseeing—assuming it does *distort* the image of the contemptible—pales in comparison to the falsehoods with which the submerged hatred and the vengefulness of the powerless take revenge against their enemies, in effigy, of course. There is too much inattentiveness, too much carelessness, too much distraction and impatience mixed in, even too much self-pleasure in the feeling of contempt for it actually to transform its object into a genuinely monstrous caricature. [. . .]

While the refined man is confident and open with himself [. . .] the resentful man is not upright or naive nor is he honest and straight with himself. His soul *squints*; his spirit loves hiding places, crawl spaces, and backdoors, everything hidden enhances *his* world, *his* security, *his* comfort. He knows all about keeping quiet, not forgetting, waiting, humbling, or deprecating himself when necessary. A race of men of resentment such as these will necessarily be *cleverer* than any refined race; it will also honor cleverness to a far greater extent, namely, as a condition of existence of the first importance. For refined men, by contrast, cleverness has something luxurious about it—it is much less important than the perfect functioning of the regulating *unconscious* instincts or even being not so clever at all, such as is the case in a bold assault at a moment of danger, against the enemy, or in the spontaneous passion of anger, love, respect, gratitude, or revenge by which refined souls have at all times recognized each other. [. . .]

Not to take seriously for very long our enemies, our misfortunes, our accidents, even our *misdeeds* is characteristic of strong, full natures in which there is an excess of the power to form, to mold, to restore, and also to forget. [. . .] Such a man shakes off with one gesture the vermin that buries itself into the bodies of other men. Here alone a genuine "*love* for your enemy" is possible—assuming such a thing is possible at all on earth. What reverence the refined man has for his enemy!—this reverence is already a step toward love. . . . After all, he demands for himself an enemy, as a mark of honor. He cannot stand an enemy other than the one in which there is nothing to despise and *everything* to honor! In contrast to this, imagine "the enemy" as conceived by the man of resentment and precisely here is his contribution, his creation: he has conceived "the evil enemy," "*the Evil One*," the basic idea from which he then derives as copy and contrast a "good one"—himself!

11

This is exactly the opposite of what the refined man does, who conceives the basic concept "good" by himself, in advance and spontaneously, and only then creates a notion "bad"! Here the "bad" as conceived by the refined man and there that "evil" conceived in the cauldron of implacable hatred—the former is something derivative, a secondary thing, a contrasting shade, the latter, by contrast, is the original, the beginning, the primary *act* in the conception of slave morality. How different are these words "bad" and "evil," particularly since they are both the opposite of what seems to be the same concept "good"! But it is *not* the same concept "good." Let us ask *who* actually is "evil" in the morality of resentment. To be blunt, it is *precisely* the "good" of the other morality, precisely those who are refined, powerful, ruling, but now repainted, reinterpreted, revised through the poisonous eye of resentment. We would be the last to deny that whoever came to know these "good men" only as enemies came to know nothing other than *evil enemies*. The same men, who are held in check by custom, respect, habit, gratitude, even more so by mutual suspicion and jealousy, who otherwise in relations with one another are so considerate, self-disciplined, tender, loyal, proud, and friendly, these men, when they turn outward, to where the strange, *the* strangers are, are not much better than wild animals released from their cages. [. . .] It is impossible to overlook the wild animal, the magnificent *blond beast* who avidly prowls in search of spoil and victory, lying at the heart of these refined races. This hidden heart needs to reveal itself from time to time; the animal needs to be released into the wilderness again: Roman, Arabian, Germanic, Japanese nobility, Homeric heroes, Scandinavian Vikings were all alike in this need. It was the refined races who left behind them the concept "barbarian" wherever they went; even their highest culture reveals the fact that they were conscious of it and proud of it (for example, when Pericles says to his Athenians in his famous funeral oration "we have forced every sea and land to be the highway of our daring, and everywhere whether for *evil* or for good, have left imperishable monuments behind us").[1] This "daring" of the refined races, mad, absurd, sudden in the way it appears; the unpredictability and even the improbability of their endeavors [. . .]; their indifference to and scorn for security, body, life, and comfort; their shocking cheerfulness and their profound delight in all destruction and in the cruel liberties of victory—all this came together, in the

[1]From Thucydides, *The Peloponnesian War*, Robert Crawley, trans. (New York: E. P. Dutton, 1950), p. 126. At the outset of the Peloponnesian War, which engulfed the Greek city-states in the fifth century BCE, Pericles, the elected leader of Athens, delivered a funeral oration for the fallen that defined the ideas of Athenian democracy and the civic virtue of Athenian power.

minds of those who suffered from it, to make up the image of the "barbarian," the "evil enemy," or of the "Goths," the "Vandals."[2] The deep, icy mistrust that even today the German arouses as soon as he comes to power is an echo of that inextinguishable horror with which for hundreds of years Europe witnessed the fury of the blond German beast. [...] We are quite justified in continuing to fear the blond beast who lies at the heart of all refined races and remaining on guard against it. But what man would not a hundred times sooner be terrified, but also admire, than *not* be terrified at all, but never be rid of the nauseating sight of what is misshapen, shriveled, wasted, and poisoned? And is this not *our* fate?

13

But let us return to the problem of the *other* origin of "good," of good as conceived by the man of resentment. [...] When the oppressed, downtrodden, and violated exhort each other in the vengeful trickery of powerlessness: "Let us be different from those who are evil, let us be good! And good is anyone who does not violate, who does not harm anyone, who does not attack, who does not retaliate, who leaves revenge to God, who keeps himself hidden as we do, who avoids all evil and, all in all, expects little from life, and like us is patient, humble, and just." What this amounts to, if you lend it a disinterested and impartial ear, is this: "The weak are just weak; it would be best if we did nothing *for which we are not strong enough*." But this sober assessment, this base cleverness, which even insects possess (when in danger, they play dead so as not "to do" too much) has, thanks to the pretension and self-deception of the powerless, dressed itself up in the ostentatious garb of an abstemious, quiet, resigned virtue as if the weakness of the weak—that is to say, their *essence*, the effects of their actions, their entire inalterable, enduring reality—amounted to a freely willed effort, something willed or chosen, an *achievement*, a *meritorious* act. This sort of man *needs* to believe in the disinterested, free "subject" out of an instinct of self-preservation and self-affirmation in which every lie becomes its own virtue. The subject (or what is commonly referred to as the *soul*) has become perhaps the most firmly established dogma on earth precisely because it makes it possible for the dying, the weak, and the oppressed everywhere to

[2] *Goths, Vandals*: Germanic peoples, vernacularly known as "the barbarians," who overran the Roman Empire in the fourth and fifth centuries.

deceive themselves and misconstrue their weakness as freedom, their so-and-so as *achievement*.

SECOND ESSAY: "GUILT," "BAD CONSCIENCE," AND THE LIKE

7

Life on earth was much more cheerful when men were not yet ashamed of their cruelty and pessimists did not yet exist. The skies darkened over men in proportion to the degree that they felt ashamed of *man*. The weary, pessimistic outlook, mistrust of the riddle of life, the ice-cold No of disgust with life—these are not the characteristics of the *most evil* period in human history; rather, they appear in the light of day when the swamp weeds that they are, when the swamp where they belong come into being—I mean the morbid sentimentalization and moralization by which the animal "man" is finally taught to be ashamed of all his instincts. On the way to becoming an "angel" (not to use a harsher word) man developed that upset stomach and pasty tongue which made not only the joy and innocence of animals nauseating but life itself repugnant so that at the sight of himself man holds his nose and stands there alongside Pope Innocent III making a catalog of his repulsive characteristics ("unclean birth, disgusting nourishment in the womb, the baseness of human flesh, a horrible smell, the secretion of spit, urine, and shit").[3] Now, when suffering is always the first of the arguments marshaled *against* existence, as its most questionable feature, it is worthwhile to remember the times when men made the opposite judgment because they were unwilling to refrain from *making* suffering and saw suffering as a great enchantment, a seductive lure *for* life itself. [. . .] What is really so outrageous about suffering is not suffering itself but the meaninglessness of suffering. Neither for Christians, who saw in suffering a whole mysterious machinery of salvation, nor for the childlike man of ancient times who saw all suffering in terms of the spectator or the perpetrator of suffering, could there be any *meaningless* suffering. In order to get rid of any latent, unseen, or unwitnessed suffering and to honestly deny

---

[3]*Pope Innocent III* (1160/61–1216): Innocent oversaw the expansion of the papacy in the Middle Ages. Here Nietzsche is referring to his book *On the Misery of the Human Condition* (circa 1200), in which Innocent describes the physical vileness of men and women, a state of degradation that only God can redeem.

it, people in the past were basically forced to invent gods and all the creatures in between heaven and hell who roamed around half hidden, could see in the dark, and rarely passed up an interesting, painful spectacle. With the help of these inventions, life then played its familiar tricks to justify itself and to justify its "evil"; today it uses other aids and inventions (for example, the riddle of life or being as a problem of knowledge). "All evil is justified if a god takes pleasure in it"—this was the logic of sentiment in prehistory, and not just in prehistory. The gods as connoisseurs of *cruel* spectacles—this age-old conception still permeates our European civilization! Just think of Calvin and Luther.[4] In any case, the *Greeks* certainly provided their gods with no more pleasing entertainment than the pleasures of cruelty. With what eyes do you think Homer[5] let his gods look down on the destinies of men? What was the ultimate meaning of the Trojan War[6] and other similar tragic atrocities? They were undoubtedly intended to be *spectacles* for the gods. [. . .] Wasn't the primary purpose of that extremely foolhardy and fateful philosophical invention, first made in Europe, of "free will," of man's absolute freedom to do good or evil, to justify the idea that the interest of the gods in men and their virtues *could never be exhausted*? On this worldly stage there was to be no lack of genuinely new things, of terrible tensions, distressing situations, and catastrophes: a completely deterministic world would have been predictable and therefore soon quite boring for the gods—reason enough, for these *friends of the gods*, the philosophers, not to have inflicted a deterministic world on them! The men of the ancient world brim with this tender regard for "the audience"; they make up an essentially public, eye-catching world in which happiness cannot be imagined without spectacles and festivals—and, as said, there is a lot spectacle to great *punishment.*

16

I take bad conscience to be a serious illness which man was bound to contract under the pressure of perhaps the most fundamental transfor-

---

[4]Martin Luther (1483–1546): The German monk and theologian whose break with the authority of the papacy in Rome ushered in the Reformation and the development of Protestantism. John Calvin (1509–1564): A French-born Protestant theologian who stressed the unknowability of God's grace.

[5]*Homer.* The ninth-century BCE Greek poet who wrote *The Iliad* and *The Odyssey.*

[6]*Trojan War.* The ten-year war waged by the Greeks against Troy, resulting from the abduction of Helen by Paris that led to the destruction of the city-state. It is the centerpiece of Homer's *Iliad.*

mation he had ever experienced—the transformation of finding himself at long last confined inside the bounds of society and peace. These half-animals, so well adapted to the wilderness, to war, to adventure, to roaming around, faced the same situation as sea animals when they were forced either to become land animals or to perish. From one moment to the next, their instincts were devalued and "set aside." They had to go on foot and "carry themselves" where before the water had carried them: an enormous weight settled on them. They felt clumsy performing the most simple tasks; they could no longer rely on their familiar guides, on the drives that had unconsciously stabilized them in this new, unknown world. The poor things were reduced to thinking, inferring, reckoning, pairing off cause and effect, depending on their "consciousness," their weakest, most fallible organ! I do not think there was ever such a feeling of misery and a leaden sense of unease on this earth! And it is not as though their instincts suddenly stopped making their demands! But it was difficult and seldom possible to give in to them: for the most part, they needed to find new gratifications underground. The instincts which are not discharged externally, *redirect themselves internally*—this is what I call the *interiorization* of man. This is the point when man acquires the growth which one later calls his "soul." This whole interior world, paper-thin at first, acquired depth, width, and height, expanded and extended itself in proportion to the *inhibition* of man's external drives. All the terrible controls by which state institutions protected themselves against the ancient instincts of freedom—including the right to punish, above all—had the result that all the instincts of wild, free-spirited men were turned around *against man himself*. Hostility, cruelty, the joy of hunting, attacking, defeating, destroying—all these instincts turned on their possessors—*this* is the origin of "bad conscience." In the absence of external enemies and outside resistance, forced into the oppressive narrowness and routine of custom, man impatiently ripped himself apart, tearing, gnawing, beating, mistreating himself; this animal who is supposed to be "tamed," rubbing itself raw against the bars of its cage; this deprived creature consumed with homesickness for the desert, forced to make out of his own self an adventure, a torture chamber, an insecure and dangerous wilderness—this prisoner consumed with despair, this fool, became the inventor of "bad conscience." He introduced the worst, most sinister illness from which humanity has not recovered: man's suffering of *man, of himself* as a result of the forced detachment of man from his animal past, the sudden descent into new living conditions, the declaration of war against all the old instincts on which his strength, lust, and audacity had up to then depended. Let us immediately, on the other hand, add that with the existence of an animal soul directed against itself, taking sides against itself, something so new, deep, unprecedented, mysterious, contradictory, and *future-filled* had appeared that the character of the earth was fundamentally transformed. Indeed, divine spectators were needed to dignify the spectacle that began then but the end of which is not yet in sight—a spectacle too subtle, too marvelous, too paradoxical for it to be played unobserved, meaninglessly on some ridiculous planet somewhere! From now on, man has to be counted *among* the most unexpected and exciting lucky throws in the game of dice played by Heraclitus's "great child," be he called Zeus or chance.[7] He arouses an interest, a sense of suspense for his part, and a measure of hope—almost a certainty—that with man something is being announced and is preparing itself, as if man were not a goal but a way, an episode, a bridge, a great promise. . . .

17

This *instinct for freedom* forcibly made latent—we have seen this already—this instinct for freedom pushed back and kicked back, incarcerated in its interiority and in the end able to discharge and release itself only on itself: this and this alone is *bad conscience* in its beginnings.

23

What follows should suffice once and for all to explain the origins of "holy God." That the conception of gods does not *in itself* necessarily lead to the degradation of the imagination [. . .], that there are *more*

[7] *Heraclitus*: An ancient Greek philosopher from the sixth century BCE whose fragmentary writings developed a philosophy of eternal, restless change that influenced Nietzsche; Nietzsche at one point refers to "my ancestors: Heraclitus, Empedocles, Spinoza, Goethe." See Walter Kaufmann, *Nietzsche: Philosopher, Psychologist, Antichrist*, 4th rev. ed. (Princeton, N.J.: Princeton University Press, 1974), p. 109. In one fragment (B 52), Heraclitus refers to a lifetime as the play of the child and the kingdom of the child, stressing both the capriciousness of the play of the gods, hence the typical Greek reference to dice, and the radical freedom of mortals, who for Nietzsche can be like the gods or children in their inventiveness. The "great child" is not Heraclitus's phrase, but is consistent with the meaning of the fragment. For the fragment, see Ludwig Winterhalder, *Das Wort Heraklits* (Erlenbach-Zurich: Eugen Rentsch, 1962), p. 62. For a discussion of the imagery of children, play, and dice, see Roman Dilcher, *Studies in Heraclitus* (Hildesheim: Georg Olms Verlag, 1995), p. 155.

refined uses for the gods than for man's self-crucifixion and self-violation in which Europe has excelled for the past millennia—this can fortunately be confirmed with just a glance at the *Greek gods*, who are the reflections of refined, masterful men in whom the *animal* in man felt divine and did *not* rip itself apart or rage against itself! For the longest time these Greeks used their gods expressly to keep "bad conscience" at a distance so that they could make the most of their freedom of the soul—the very opposite of the way Christianity makes use of its God. They went *very far*, these marvelous, lion-hearted children. And no less an authority than the Zeus of Homer lets it be known that they are making it too easy for themselves. "Strange!" he says at one point—the case is that of Aegisthus, a *very* bad case—

> how shameless, the way these mortals blame the gods. *From us alone*, they say, *come all their miseries*, yes, but they themselves, with their own reckless ways, compound their pains beyond their proper share.[8]

We can immediately hear and see that this Olympian spectator and judge has no intention of holding a grudge against them or thinking badly of them. "How *foolish* they are!" he considers the misdeeds of mortal men—and "foolishness," "ignorance," a little "crazy in the head," this much the Greeks of the strongest, bravest age had *conceded* about themselves in order to explain many bad and calamitous things. Foolishness, *not* sin! Do you understand that? . . . Still, this craziness in the head was a problem—"how is it at all possible? where did it come from, with heads like the ones *we* have, we fortunate men of noble origin, happy, well-endowed, well-born, virtuous and refined?"—for hundreds of years the refined Greek asked himself this question in the face of any incomprehensible atrocity or outrage with which one of his peers had polluted himself. "It must have been a *god* who confused him," he finally answered, shaking his head. . . . This conclusion is *typical* for the Greeks. . . . In this way, the gods served to justify man, even in his wickedness; they served as causes of evil—in

---

[8]From Homer, *The Odyssey*, Robert Fagles, trans. (New York: Penguin, 1996), p. 78 (1, 36–40). *Aegisthus*: In Homer's *Odyssey*, written in the ninth century BCE, Zeus, the father of all the gods in ancient Greek mythology, reflects on the excessive suffering that mortals bring upon themselves, referring in this case to the warnings that Aegisthus received not to have an affair with Clytemnestra, the wife of Agamemnon, who was away leading the Greek armies in the Trojan War. The lovers kill Agamemnon upon his return and Aegisthus is, in turn, murdered seven years later by Agamemnon's son, Orestes.

those days, they did not punish themselves, but rather, and this is *more refined*, they took the blame.

24

I shall conclude with three question marks, it seems. You might ask me: "What are you really doing here, erecting an ideal or smashing one?" ... But have you asked yourselves adequately how much the erection of *every* ideal on earth has cost? How much reality has had to be falsified and distorted as a result, how many lies sanctified, how much conscience disrupted, how much "god" had to be sacrificed every time? For a temple to be erected, *a temple has to be smashed*: that is the law—give me an example where that has not been the case! ... For thousands of years, men have been racking their consciences and otherwise torturing themselves: we modern men are their heirs. We have been practicing this for a long time, this is our talent perhaps; in any case, we have become very used to it and very good at it. For too long, man has regarded his natural inclinations with an "evil eye" so that they finally became intertwined with his "bad conscience." To attempt the opposite would *in itself* be possible, but who has the strength for that?—namely, to intertwine with bad conscience all the *unnatural* inclinations, the longing for the beyond and for all the things that resist sense, instinct, nature, animals, in short all the existing ideals that negate life and slander the world. To whom should we turn with *such* aspirations and demands? ... Of course, we would have the *good* men against us. The same goes for the comfortable, the self-satisfied, the vain, the sentimental, and the weary. ... What gives greater offense and turns people off than to reveal some of the severity and high-mindedness with which we treat ourselves? And yet— how accommodating and friendly the world is when we act like everyone else does and "go with the flow" like everyone else does! ... Very *different* spirits would be required to attain this goal, which in our day and age is unlikely: spirits strengthened through wars and victories, for whom conquest, adventure, danger, and pain have actually become necessities. They would have to tolerate the thinner air of great heights, winter journeys, and mountains and ice in every sense. They would need a kind of sublime wickedness, a supremely self-confident playful mind, which is part of being healthy. It would require, just this: *great health!* ... Is this still possible today? ... But someday, in an age stronger than this rotten, self-doubting present day, he will have to come to us, the *redeeming* man of great love and great contempt, the creative spirit whose surging strength continually keeps him from being driven into the distance or into the beyond, whose solitude will be misunderstood by the people as a flight *from* reality, when he has really only immersed and steeped himself and sunk *into* reality so that one day, when he comes to light again, he can *redeem* this reality, redemption from the curse that the previously existing ideal had put on it. This man of the future, who will not only redeem us from the old ideal but from the great nausea, the will to nothingness, and nihilism *that was bound to grow out of it.* The ringing of the bells at noon, the great decision that once again liberates the will and gives back to the earth its purpose and to men their hope, this anti-Christ and anti-nihilist, this victor over God and nothingness—*he must come one day.*

THIRD ESSAY: WHAT DO ASCETIC IDEALS MEAN?

28

Aside from ascetic ideals, man, the *animal* that is man, does not have any meaning so far. His existence on earth has no purpose. "What is man for, actually?"—this was a question without an answer. There was no *will* for man and earth; behind every great human destiny sounded the even louder refrain, "so what!" Just *this* is what the ascetic ideal meant: something was *missing*, man was surrounded by an enormous *void*—he did not know how to justify, to explain, to affirm himself. He *suffered* from the problem of his meaning. As it was, he was essentially an animal that *suffered*. But suffering itself was *not* his problem, but the fact that his cries of "*why* do I suffer?" did not bring forth an answer. As the bravest of the animals and most accustomed to suffering, man does *not* reject suffering: he *desires* it, he even seeks it out, provided the *meaning* of suffering, the *purpose* of suffering has been revealed to him. Up to now, man has been cursed by the meaninglessness of suffering, *not* suffering itself—*and so the ascetic ideal provided man meaning!* It was the only meaning, but any meaning is better than none at all. The ascetic ideal was in every respect the "*faute de mieux*" [for lack of anything better] par excellence. In it, suffering was *laid out* to be contemplated, the tremendous emptiness seemed filled out, the door to any suicidal nihilism shut. This laying out—there can be no doubt—prompted new suffering, deeper, more inward, more poisonous, suffering that gnawed at life: it put all suffering into the perspective of *guilt*. . . . Nonetheless—man was thereby *saved*, he had a *meaning*, he was no longer a leaf in the wind, the plaything of the absurd, of "non-sense." From now on he could *will* something—no matter what, why, and how he did it at first, *the will itself was saved.* We need hardly conceal from ourselves *what* was expressed by this will which took its direction from the ascetic ideal: the hatred of what made us human, and even more of what made us animal, and more still hatred of the material, this aversion to the senses, to reason itself, this fear of happiness and beauty, this longing to get away from all appearances, all change, all becoming, all death, all wishing, to get away from longing itself—all this means, let us dare to grasp it, a *will to nothingness*, a counterwill to life, a revolt against the fundamental conditions of life, but nonetheless it is and remains a *will!* . . . And, to say it in conclusion what I have said in the beginning: man would rather will *nothingness* than *not* will. . . .

A Friedrich Nietzsche Chronology
(1844–1903)

1844 Nietzsche is born in Röcken, Germany, on October 15.

1849 Nietzsche's father, a Lutheran pastor, dies.

1864 Nietzsche begins his studies in classical philology at Bonn University.

1865 Nietzsche continues his studies at Leipzig University.

1868 Nietzsche first meets the composer Richard Wagner.

1869 Nietzsche is appointed professor at the University of Basel, Switzerland.

1873 The first of his four *Untimely Meditations* is published.

1874 "On the Uses and Disadvantages of History for Life," the second, as well as the third of his *Untimely Meditations* is published.

1876 Nietzsche breaks with Wagner; the fourth and final of Nietzsche's *Untimely Meditations* is published.

1878 *Human, All Too Human* is published.

1879 Nietzsche resigns his post at Basel.

1882 *The Gay Science* is published.

1883 Nietzsche begins *Thus Spoke Zarathustra*; parts 1 and 2 are published.

1884 Nietzsche writes and publishes part 3 of *Thus Spoke Zarathustra*.

1885 Nietzsche writes and publishes part 4 of *Thus Spoke Zarathustra*.

1886 Nietzsche publishes *Beyond Good and Evil*.

1887 Nietzsche publishes *On the Genealogy of Morals*.

1889 In Turin, Italy, Nietzsche falls into an incurable madness at the beginning of January; he is ultimately released into the care of his mother in Naumburg, Germany.

1897 Nietzsche's mother dies, and his sister moves Nietzsche to Weimar, Germany.

1900 Nietzsche dies in Weimar on August 25.

1903 "On Truths and Lies in an Extramoral Sense" (1873) is published in the first comprehensive edition of Nietzsche's collected works.

Questions for Consideration

1. What is the importance that Nietzsche puts on the distinction between "the death of God" and the murder of God?

2. In *Beyond Good and Evil*, what does Nietzsche mean by "simplification" when he comments on the free spirits or the origins of language, and what are the implications?

3. Why do the free spirits wear masks? (See *Beyond Good and Evil*.)

4. What does Nietzsche mean by his many references to cruelty?

5. In what way does truth rest on error? Is error a sign of life?

6. Do Nietzsche's supermen and free spirits require the subordination of most other people in order to prosper? Or is Nietzsche's philosophy available to everyone? How would societies use Nietzsche's philosophy in a different manner than individual people would use it?

7. According to Nietzsche, what are the origins of sin and what role has sin played in life?

8. In what ways is the revaluation of morality two thousand years ago life enhancing, in Nietzsche's view?

9. How do the camel, the lion, and the child, in Nietzsche's sketch, "On the Three Metamorphoses" in *Thus Spoke Zarathustra*, approach knowledge and life, and how do those approaches compare to Nietzsche's views on history in "The Uses and Disadvantages of History for Life"?

10. How does Nietzsche account for the origins of the individual, what are the limits of individuality, and how are they related to the ideal of the superman?

11. Is Nietzsche's philosophy compatible with democracy? Is it helpful to conceptualize a good and just society?

Selected Bibliography

NIETZSCHE'S WRITINGS

Kaufmann, Walter, ed. and trans. *The Portable Nietzsche*. New York: Viking, 1954.

Nietzsche, Friedrich. *Beyond Good and Evil*, Walter Kaufmann, trans. New York: Random House, 1966.

Nietzsche, Friedrich. *Daybreak*, R. J. Hollingdale, trans. Cambridge: Cambridge University Press, 1997.

Nietzsche, Friedrich. *The Gay Science*, Walter Kaufmann, trans. New York: Vintage, 1974.

Nietzsche, Friedrich. *Human, All Too Human*, R. J. Hollingdale, trans. Cambridge: Cambridge University Press, 1996.

Nietzsche, Friedrich. *On the Genealogy of Morals* and *Ecce Homo*, Walter Kaufmann, trans. New York: Random House, 1967.

Nietzsche, Friedrich. *Thus Spoke Zarathustra*, Walter Kaufmann, trans. New York: Viking, 1966.

Nietzsche, Friedrich. *Untimely Meditations*, R. J. Hollingdale, trans. Cambridge: Cambridge University Press, 1997.

BIOGRAPHIES AND INTERPRETATIONS OF NIETZSCHE

Allison, David B. *Reading the New Nietzsche*. New York: Rowman & Littlefield, 2001.

Chamberlain, Leslie. *Nietzsche in Turin*. New York: Picador, 1996.

Danto, Arthur. *Nietzsche as Philosopher*. New York: Macmillan, 1965.

Hollingdale, R. J. *Nietzsche: The Man and His Philosophy*, rev. ed. Cambridge: Cambridge University Press, 1999.

Kaufmann, Walter. *Nietzsche: Philosopher, Psychologist, Antichrist*, 4th rev. ed. Princeton, N.J.: Princeton University Press, 1974.

Nehamas, Alexander. *Nietzsche: Life as Literature*. Cambridge, Mass.: Harvard University Press, 1985.

Rorty, Richard. *Contingency, Irony, and Solidarity*. Cambridge: Cambridge University Press, 1989.

Safranski, Rüdiger. *Nietzsche*, Shelley Frisch, trans. New York: Norton, 2002.

Index

adventurous spirit, 62–63
Aegisthus, 157
Agamemnon, 157*n*
animals
  consciousness of, 77
  humans as, 133–34, 147, 155–56, 159
  unhistoric nature of, 53, 56
anthropomorphization, 70–71
anti-Christ, 159
antiquarian history, 52, 57, 61–64
anti-Semitism, 3, 35, 66
aphorisms
  contradictions and, 43
  defined, 7, 43
  Nietzsche's use of, 7, 66
Aphorisms (Nietzsche), 43–47
aristocracy. *See also* nobility; refined men
  breeding, 141–43
  corruption and, 137
  equality and, 138
  language and, 138
  morality and, 123, 142
  Nietzsche's appeal to, 5
  origins of, 136–37
  religious, 147–48
  role of, 137–38
art history, monumental, 60–61
Aryans, 30, 35
Aschheim, Steven, 35
atheists, 6, 9
Athens, 30
Augustine of Hippo, 26

bad. *See also* good and bad morality system
  evil *vs.,* 151
  meaning of, 139, 151
  refined men and, 151
bad conscience, 26, 154–56
  about natural human inclinations, 159
  about unnatural human inclinations,
    159

Greek gods and, 157
  origins of, 155–56
barbarians, 152*n*
  aristocracy and, 137
  refined men and, 151–52
  resentment against, 23, 25
Beyond Good and Evil (Nietzsche), 1, 7, 13,
    121–44, 161
Bible, 79
bieder, 29
Blanqui, Auguste, 132*n*
blessed islands, 103–6
blind men, 106
"blond beast," 30
bonhomme, un, 141
Borgia, Cesare, 27–29
Buddha, 70
Buddhism, 126, 133
Burckhardt, Jacob, 62

Calvin, John, 154
camel, 32, 96
child
  as free spirit, 33
  metamorphosis of, 97–98
  myth creation and, 31, 32–33
  symbolism of, 32–33, 98
children
  alternate lifeways for, 12
  history and, 116
  imagery of, 157*n*
  sacrifice of firstborn, 112
Christ, Jesus, 67
Christianity. *See also* religion
  ancient Greece and, 29
  aphorisms, 46–47
  arrogance of, 128
  as Asian religion, 67*n*
  in Europe, 127–28
  Jews and, 67–68
  Nietzsche's criticism of, 1, 5–6, 14

165

168

myth creation (*cont.*)
  child and, 32–34
  culture and, 15
  as quality of being human, 18
  "three metamorphoses" and, 32–34
  truth and, 19
  value of, 35
  Wagner and, 34
Myth of the Twentieth Century (Rosenberg), 35

Napoleon Bonaparte, 27, 129
nations, nationalism, 34, 66–67
nature, 122–23, 136
Nazis, 5, 30, 35–36
neighbor, 129–30
Niebuhr, Barthold George, 62
Nietzsche, Friedrich
  anti-Semitism and, 3, 35
  biography, 1–3
  birth of, 2
  character of, 2
  chronology, 161–62
  death of, 2
  education of, 2
  family, 2
  influence of, 2, 3–8
  insanity of, 1, 2, 161
  legacy of, 34–37
  morality philosophy, 27–29
  Nazis and, 5, 30, 35–36
  philosophical views of, 8–34
  writings
    Aphorisms, 43–47
    Beyond Good and Evil, 121–44
    Gay Science, The, 68–79
    On the Genealogy of Morals, 144–60
    Human, All Too Human, 66–68
    Thus Spoke Zarathustra, 79–121
    On Truth and Lies in an Extramoral Sense, 47–51
    On the Uses and Disadvantages of History for Life, 51–65
  writing style, 7
nihilism, 12, 159
nobility, 115–16. *See also* aristocracy; refined men
  French, 137
  good and, 146–47
  love and, 141
  truth and, 139
norms
  in ancient Greece, 21
  overturning, 30
  polytheism and, 72–73

Odysseus, 136
Odyssey (Homer), 157n
Oedipus, 136
"Of Old and New Tablets" (Nietzsche), 79

On the Genealogy of Morals (Nietzsche), 7, 13, 23, 25, 27, 144–60, 161
  First Essay: "Good and Evil," "Good and Bad," 145–53
  Second Essay: "Guilt," "Bad Conscience," and the Like, 145, 153–59
  Third Essay: What Do Ascetic Ideals Mean?, 145, 159–60
On the Misery of the Human Condition (Innocent III), 153n
"On the Three Metamorphoses" (Nietzsche), 80, 96–98
On Truth and Lies in an Extramoral Sense (Nietzsche), 47–51, 162
On the Uses and Disadvantages of History for Life (Nietzsche), 34, 51–65
Orestes, 157n
Origin of the Species, The (Darwin), 14
overman, 29–34. *See also* superman

parables, 24
Pascal, Blaise, 26, 128
Peloponnesian War, 30, 151n
Peloponnesian War, The (Thucydides), 151n
Pericles, 151
perspectivism, 6, 35
  consciousness and, 77–78
  "God is dead" philosophy and, 9
pessimism, 153
phenomenology, 77
philophasters, 132
philosophers
  egos of, 48
  free spirits and, 125–26
  new, 12, 133
  truth and, 125
pity
  acts based on, 130
  attachment and, 124–25
  for God, 132
  morality and, 132–33, 139–40
  superman and, 85
plastic powers, 12
  of culture, 52, 55
  of humans, 55
Platonic thinking, 16
Polybius, 58
polytheism, 21–22
  in ancient Greece, 21
  benefits of, 72–73
  norms and, 72–73
  value of, 22
Protestant Reformation, 27

racial mixing, in Europe, 66–67
racism, 5
reason, superman and, 85
redemption, 106–10, 111, 116, 149, 158–59